For Cindy

45115

Brevet Amai
Feb 17, 1970
from Word free

FOY VALENTINE

A member of the Baptist World Alliance's
standing committee on religious liberty
and human rights, Dr. Valentine is
President of the Inter-Agency Council of
the Southern Baptist Convention, a
member of the Executive Committee of
Protestants and Others United for
Separation of Church and State.
In 1966, he was the special lecturer on
Christian Social Ethics for the summer
school of the International Baptist
Theological Seminary at Ruschlikon,
Switzerland.
As director of the Christian Life
Commission of the Southern Baptist
Convention, Dr. Valentine gives direction
to a program designed to help Baptists
carry the whole gospel of Christ into every
area of life. The Commission renders its
ministry in the field of applied
Christianity in the general area of: family
life, race relations, moral issues, daily work,
and Christian citizenship.

THE CROSS IN THE MARKETPLACE

THE
CROSS in the
MARKETPLACE

by

FOY VALENTINE

WORD BOOKS **WACO, TEXAS**

PREFACE

I am grateful to the Crescent Hill Baptist Church of Louisville, Kentucky, and to the pastor, Dr. John Claypool, whose invitation to deliver the messages in their first annual Weatherspoon Week provided the occasion for pulling this material together in the present form. Dr. J. B. Weatherspoon, longtime professor of preaching and Christian social ethics, gave inspiration and leadership to multitudes over decades at the point of Christian social concern; and though he is now gone, he still speaks.

Some of the material appearing here has also been used in various preaching assignments from Texas to Switzerland. The chapter on race appeared originally in the *Southwestern Journal of Theology*, April, 1965. Part of the chapter on the moral crisis was first prepared for *The Baptist Training Union Magazine* and is here reproduced with the kind permission of the Baptist Sunday School Board. The last chapter, "You Can't Go Home Again," was preached to an annual meeting of the Southern Baptist Convention and was subsequently printed in Paul Butler's *Best Sermons Volume IX*.

Originality is not claimed for the book. It represents a compilation of various materials from more than thirteen years of full time activity in the field of applied Christianity. It is submitted in the earnest hope that it will be of some help in positionizing the cross as a proper symbol not only for Christian church buildings but also for the Christian in the marketplace.

Foy Valentine

CONTENTS

Chapter 1, "The Cross in the Marketplace" 9

Chapter 2, "Revealed Religion and Social Action" . 19

Chapter 3, "The Church and the World" 43

Chapter 4, "A Christian Looks at the
                    Communist Threat" . . 57

Chapter 5, "Christians and the Current
                     Racial Crisis" . . 75

Chapter 6, "The New Morality in Christian
                     Perspective" . . 95

Chapter 7, "You Can't Go Home Again" 111

CHAPTER 1

The Cross in the Marketplace

"This is the age
Of the half-read page.
And the quick hash
And the mad dash.
The bright night
With the nerves tight.
The plane hop
With the brief stop.
The lamp tan
In a short span.
The Big Shot
In a good spot.
And the brain strain
And the heart pain.
And the cat naps
Till the spring snaps—
And the fun's done!"

[Virginia Brasier, *Saturday Evening Post*, ed. Ben Hibbs (Philadelphia: Curtis Publishing Co., May 28, 1949), p. 72.]

This may not be great poetry, but it is a reasonably accurate portrayal of the age in which we live.

This age, like every age, is an age that tries men's souls. It is an age of dry eyes, hard noses, and cold feet. It was once just at sixes and sevens but now it is at twelves and fourteens. It follows the wind; it embraces the darkness; it loves a vacuum. Its beatitude is "Blessed are the smooth for they shall never be wrinkled."

It indulges in a myopic narcissism over its own wonderful works—split atoms and a few tons of tin which it has hung on nothing. It proposes fantastically expensive voyages into space without the foggiest notion as to what to do with the space it already has. It overeats, overdrinks, overworks, and overplays so that its immoderation is known unto all men. It walks delicately, thinks slovenly, lives dully, sleeps poorly, and wakes up tired.

It is better acquainted with name-brands than it is with firebrands. It knows more about the bomb that it does about the Bible. It understands the infernal possibilities of hydrogen better than the infinite potentialities of heaven. It actually talks more about calories than it does about Christ. It has grown fat feeding on fingernails. It is an age of Thunderbolts, Thunderbirds, and Thunderballs. It knows well the 007 syndrome.

It is the age of grown men wrapped in intellectual swaddling clothes, of Christians who spoon one another lukewarm pablum in preference to the meat of strong doctrine. This is the age of the Beefed-up Big Brother and of 1984 before 1970. It is a gadget-filled paradise suspended in a hell of insecurity. It is the age of unexamined concepts, limp images, and limber lips. It moves easily from unsupportable hypotheses to foregone conclusions.

It is the age of calculated irrelevance in political campaigns—and in many an ecclesiastical empire. It is the age of the fast buck, the goof-off, the fixed price, the half-done job, the accommodated moral standard, the proximate solution, the interim ethic, the smooth cliché, a bottomless relativism, and the "new morality" which, as it is being interpreted by many, is as old as the serpent in the Garden. It fills its tank with high-octane hypocrisy from which it gets understandably poor mileage. It loves the simple purity of well-ordered confusion. It is as far from real repentance for its sin as a faith-healer is from the Mayo Clinic and it knows as little about true faith in Jesus Christ as a downtown tomcat knows about *Good Housekeeping* magazine.

It knows intimately the heavy legacy of hatred and it still responds to the demagogue's intoxicating oratory. It experiences great difficulty in distinguishing between the white horse of victory and the pale horse of death, so vast is its confusion.

It has a limited vision of poverty, but it has an unlimited poverty of vision. It is like ancient Israel of whom it was said, "The word of the Lord was rare in those days; there was no frequent vision" (I Samuel 3:1 RSV). It is the age of cheap grace where sinners have been called to Christ without being called to bring forth social fruits "meet for repentance."

Its loins are girt about with half-truth; it bears the breastplate of self-righteousness; its feet are shod with the bad news of preparation for war; it clutches the shield of doubt; it wears the helmet of damnation; and it wields the sword of the flesh.

In this time of agonizing reappraisal when the question, "What's wrong?" is on a vast multitude of lips both in the nation and in the Christian fellowship, let us ask the prior questions: "Where is God?" "Who am I?" "What shall we do?"

When Bildad, Eliphaz, and Zophar were giving their inadequate answers, Job was asking the important questions. Perhaps this age also can profit by asking again the important questions: "Where is God?" "Who am I?" "What shall we do?"

I. WHERE IS GOD?

(1) God is in history effecting man's salvation. He is in creation, in Adam and in Eve, in Noah, in Abraham and in Sarah, in Isaac and in Jacob, in Moses, in Isaiah and in Amos, in the law and in the prophets, in the cradle of Bethlehem, and on the cross at Calvary. But God is not only in ancient history. He is in modern history as well—in the Reformation, in the nailing of Martin Luther's ninety-five theses to the door of Castle Church in Wittenberg, in the three intrepid little sailboats of Christopher Columbus, in Africa's bold step into the Twentieth Century, in the halls of the United Nations where men are trying to learn the gray art of shouting at one another instead of the black art of shooting at one another, in today's human affairs, conference rooms, crossroads, and marketplaces. God is not simply There and Then. God is Here and Now, the great "I am that I am," beyond history, before history, over history, under history, and in history. And Christ's gospel of redemption, His good news of salvation, came not only to the shepherds in the Judaean hills in an agrarian world two thousand years ago. His gospel has come to this age also.

History is not just something unpleasant that happens to other folks. History happens to everybody. And history is now happening to you and me. There is no justification for our standing here shuffling our feet and wringing our hands and crying and cutting ourselves with knives and neurotically hunting scapegoats. God is in history. Our sovereign God is in history effecting man's salvation; and Christians ought to feel a wonderful security, a glorious liberty, and a peace that passes all understanding in this knowledge. As the winds of change blow with their devastating fury across the face of all the earth, let us trust the God who is in history, for He is in our history also. If we are true to God, He will not forsake us; and if we are not true to Him, no amount of histrionics will throw the Hounds of Heaven off our trail.

(2) Where is God? God is in Christ reconciling the world unto Himself. To say that God is in Christ is to affirm that Jesus Christ our Lord is the Word by whom the worlds were made, the Lamb slain from the foundation of the world, the Messiah of Old Testament prophecy, in the fullness of time a perfect man and every whit a man, and the Author, Sustainer, and Finisher of our faith. To say that God in Christ is reconciling the world to Himself is to say that Christ's reconciling work is past, present, and future. It is past in the sense that Christ has reconciled the believing sinner and the heavenly Father. It is present in the sense that men, through Christ, are being reconciled to their estranged families, separated parents, distrusting children, and alienated fellow men. It is future in the sense that we shall know complete conformity to Christ who loved us and gave Himself for us, for Christ who has begun the work of grace in us will assuredly complete it in His own time. Jesus Christ is not just King of Kings and Lord of Lords in Handel's "Messiah." He is King of Lyndon B. Johnson and Lord of Mao Tse-Tung. He is

King of Harold Wilson and Lord of Fidel Castro.

Our world has had a great fall and not all of the Free World's horses or all of communism's men can put it together again. This is the work of God who is in Christ reconciling the world unto Himself.

(3) Where is God? God is in church. Charles Haddon Spurgeon said, "I do not believe in salvation outside the pale of the church." And if we will not hear Spurgeon then let us hear Jesus who said, "On this rock I will build my church and the gates of hell shall not prevail against it" (Matthew 16:18), and Paul who said that Christ "loved the church and gave himself for it" (Ephesians 5:25). To say that God and His great salvation are one thing and church membership quite another thing, a mere optional matter for individuals to take or leave, is to inject into revealed religion an element of prickly individualism which fractures the gospel and fragments the New Testament. The church is the body of Christ, the bride of Christ, the building of Christ. It is the *ecclesia* of God distinguished by fellowship, service, and proclamation—*koinonia, diakonia,* and *kerugma*—brothering, helping, and preaching. As men must have community or be less than men, so Christians must have the church or be less than the people of God. It is infinitely more important, moreover, for Christians to *be* the church than it is for them simply to attend church, build the church, support the church, give to the church, or serve the church. Christians who grasp this idea that they *are* the church understand that Christianity must be demonstrated before it is declared, that it must be done before it can be taught, that it must be practiced before it is preached.

Where is God? God is in history; God is in Christ; and God is in church.

II. WHO AM I?

At the graveside of Willie Loman in Arthur Miller's "Death of a Salesman," one of the sons, Biff, standing by, says with rare discernment, "He never knew who he was." [Arthur Miller, *Death of a Salesman* (New York: The Viking Press, 1949), p. 138.] Is not this the essence of tragedy? The need to know who we are, to be somebody, to have a name is as deep as life. In these times there are many hindrances to self-identification: the uprooting of families by moves so frequent that sociologists say there has never before in history been as much voluntary migration as there is in the United States today, the lack of leisure, the paucity of sanctuary, and the absence of father and family and friends and kinfolks to help provide the answer to the great question, "Who am I?"

(1) Who am I? I am a man made in the image of God, after His spiritual, rational, moral likeness. The image of God is man. It is because of this that I must insist that I am not America's man or the South's man or capitalism's man or free enterprise's man or labor's man or management's man or the Democrat's man or the Republican's man but God's man.

(2) Who am I? I am a Christian, bought "and at what a price" (I Corinthians 6:20 Phillips). Because Christ died for me and because He loves me, I have infinite value as does every other human being on earth. It is in encounter with the living God through repentance and faith in Jesus Christ as Lord that I become a whole man, and it is only after this encounter that I can tell you, really, who I am; and it is in this encounter alone that mankind in quest of its true identity can come to itself, find its name, and be somebody.

(3) Who am I? I am responsible. I am a responsible Christian man. Every moral decision of my life I am constrained to make in the light of who I am. It is as a responsible Christian man that I must make decisions about family life, race relations, daily work, citizenship, and the specific moral issues which always dog the feet of moral man. God's basic concern is not that Christians should combat successfully the specific family problems of teen-age marriages, the breakdown of authority in the home, divorce, and aging, but that Christians *should want to* confront these issues in the mind and spirit of Christ. His first concern is not that Christians should bury Jim Crow but that they *should want to* bury Jim Crow; not that Christians should transform politics but that they *should want to* transform politics; not that they should conquer alcohol but that they *should want to* conquer alcohol; not that they should defeat gambling but that they *should want to* defeat gambling— *because of who they are.* When God says, "Be ye holy for I am holy" (I Peter 1:16), he is actually saying, "Be my people for I am your God." Be righteous because God is righteous. Be right because God is right. Be responsible because God is responsible.

III. WHAT SHALL WE DO?

We are in no position to ask, "What shall we do?" until we have first asked, "Where is God?" and "Who am I?" When these two prior questions have been asked and answered, however, then the one, great, overpowering question remaining is "What shall we do?" Having become, by God's grace, the people we ought to be, we can by the power of His might do the work we ought to do.

With George MacLeod, "I am recovering the claim

that Jesus was not crucified in a cathedral between two candles, but on a cross between two thieves; on the town garbage-heap; at a crossroad so cosmopolitan that they had to write His title in Hebrew and in Latin and in Greek (or shall we say in English, in Bantu and in Afrikaans?); at the kind of place where cynics talk smut, and thieves curse, and soldiers gamble. Because that is where He died. And that is what He died about. And that is where churchmen should be and what churchmanship should be about." [*Only One Way Left* (Glasgow: The Iona Community, 1956), p. 38.]

What shall we do? We shall renew our vows to God: We shall not forsake the assembling of ourselves together as is the manner of some. We shall be good stewards of all that we have and are and hope to be. We shall preach the gospel. We shall not wince at the scandal of the cross. We shall be swimmers against tides. We shall remember that unless a grain of wheat fall into the ground and die, it abides alone (John 12:24), and that if any man will come after Christ, he must deny himself and take up his cross daily and follow Him (Luke 9:23).

We shall match our disenchantment with the present age with a patient effort to change it. We shall add our Christian salt to the fresh, red meat that is our present world lest the maggots of mammon infect and ruin it. We shall shine our lights in a dim and gloomy world where without them men would continue to stumble piteously and fall painfully in the dark.

Knowing that the disembodied, unformed Word is no Word at all, we shall again let the Word be flesh so that the love of God is expressed through our changed lives in a language men can understand. We shall recognize that social involvement is not an optional matter of ethical obedience but a condition of being in communion with God at all. We shall understand that to be hid with God in Christ is not to wallow in glossolalia but to be rightly involved in community. We shall quit singing, "Far away the noise of strife upon my ear is falling. . . . Safe am I within the Castle of God's word retreating . . . for I am dwelling in Beulah land," and start singing, "Rescue the perishing; care for the dying; snatch them in pity from sin and the grave," and "Where Cross the Crowded Ways of Life."

We shall return to a concern for people with the assurance that as we do our religion will burst gloriously into new life.

We shall remember that Paul nearly always commenced his epistles with piety and climaxed them with politics.

We shall know again the heady, hearty, holy thrill of moral leadership. We shall stand in the bow of the ship as it cuts its way into the uncharted sea of a new world order.

We shall not mythologize the pivotal point of the Christian gospel: that the essence of the heavenly Father's majesty is Jesus Christ's magnificently successful humanity. We shall feed the hungry, heal the brokenhearted, set at liberty them that are bruised, clothe the naked, release the prisoners from bondage, and preach the gospel to the poor. We shall recover the fullness of the gospel. We shall acknowledge the claim of Christ on all of life. We shall own Him Lord.

What shall we do? We shall raise again the cross in the marketplace for this is where God is, this is who we all are, and this is what we must do.

CHAPTER 2

Revealed Religion and Social Action

Daniel Defoe, in his masterpiece, *Robinson Crusoe,* weaves a fascinating tale of one man alone on a secluded island. The story progresses quite satisfactorily with the lonely Crusoe all by himself until the author is ready to move toward the story's climax. It is then that another man, Friday, is brought by the discerning Defoe into the picture. Then, after Friday, there are still others who come until finally when the book closes, Robinson Crusoe is once again surrounded by a web of human relationships. Defoe would have been hard put to have made a satisfactory story out of a Crusoe who lived absolutely and permanently to himself.

The fact is that no man lives to himself and no man dies to himself.

Old Testament Revelation and Social Action

In the beginning God made man a creature for community. Seeing that it was not good for man to be alone, God made for Adam "an helpmeet" and then commanded the two of them to multiply and replenish the earth. God has spoken clearly, both in the kind of man He created and in what His written Word specifically says, concerning the social nature and social obligations of man. The Lord has been concerned from the beginning about man's relationship to his fellow men.

Old Testament revelation portrays an ethical God who, unlike the pagan deities—Zeus, Pan, Baal, Diana, Ashtaroth, and their like—is the essence of moral rectitude Himself, and who stringently requires uncompromised righteousness of His people, both personally and in their social relationships.

While the Old Testament clearly speaks to today's world concerning social responsibility and social action, it is approached with the understanding that God's revelation of Himself is not complete except in Christ.

Several underlying concepts are helpful in understanding social action in the Old Testament. The first of these is the Old Testament concept of a personal God. The Jews understood, though dimly at times, that their God, who was a person, could never approve of their treating other persons simply as means to an end rather than as ends in themselves. The teaching of the Old Testament is that every person, because he is made in the image of a personal God, has infinite worth. This tempers the valid statement of Albert C. Knudson that "human life was always a community life. And the farther we go back, the more marked does the solidarity of the family, clan, and other social groups become. The individual tends to lose himself in larger wholes. Society, not the individual, becomes the object of primary concern." [*The Religious Teaching of the Old Testament* (New York: Abingdon-Cokesbury, 1918), p. 316.] The revelation of the Old Testament shows plainly that we are not persons only, but persons-in-relationship, both to God and to society.

The second underlying concept which is helpful in gaining an understanding of the place of social action in the Old Testament is that of sin. A. B. Davidson says that sin in the Old Testament is ". . . usually of two kinds: either *forsaking* of Jehovah, God of Israel, or social wrongdoing of the members of the Covenant people to one another." [*The Theology of the Old Testament* (New York: Charles Scribner's Sons, 1920), p. 213.] While the Psalmist could cry out, "Against thee only have I sinned," he well knew the consequences of sin in the larger community. All sin is sin against God, but no sin is void of social consequences as David's experience dramatically illustrates.

There are several Old Testament words for sin. One of these means "to miss the mark, to fail"; another means "perversity, iniquity"; another means "transgression, to trespass"; and still another, "evil." These meanings apply first to God and then to others in the community. For instance, while a believer may miss the mark regarding his financial stewardship to God, he may also miss the mark regarding his own duties in the area of citizenship within his community. And while an individual may act perversely and iniquitously toward God, he may also so act toward his fellow man. While God may observe evil in a man's heart, men may observe that evil as it is expressed through such means as the sale of beverage alcohol and the exploitation of the poor. Indeed, sin is both Godward and manward.

A third underlying concept in this brief look at the Old Testament and social action is that of the neighbor. This concept is generally limited in Old Testament times, though not so much as is sometimes supposed, to the immediate community. The word "neighbor" occurs 136 times in the Old Testament, which has in the original language five different words so translated. One word translated "neighbor" means "equal, fellow"; another means "near one"; another means "female friend, companion"; another "dweller, inhabitant"; and still another, "friend, companion." While this last word is by far the most commonly used word for "neighbor" in the Old Testament, the basic revelation at this point is that God's people are to concern themselves with the needs of those about them, not being satisfied to live to themselves.

With these three underlying concepts in mind, let us look at some actual cases of social action in the Old Testament.

When God dealt with Cain, he did so on the basis that he was his brother's keeper (Genesis 4:9-12).

God loved Abraham and blessed him saying, "I know him, that he will command his children and his household after him, and they shall keep the way of the Lord, to do justice and judgment" (Genesis 18:19). God chose Abraham in the knowledge that he would teach his children to walk in righteousness in their larger social relationships.

"Moses," Charles Foster Kent says, "is the first man in history with a well-developed social consciousness." [*The Social Teachings of the Prophets and Jesus* (New York: Charles Scribner's Sons, 1917), p. 7.] Perhaps this evaluation of Moses cannot be defended. At any rate, however, Moses was vitally concerned with social action, and he developed some very effective methods of getting the community of Israel to act. As Kent suggests, he first educated the people, gathering together all the elders of Israel (Exodus 4:29-31). Later he organized them for united action. Then he formulated and presented to Pharaoh the just demands of the community. When those demands were refused he resorted to practical agitation. And then, having exhausted these methods, he waited patiently and persistently for the outworking of the social and economic laws through which the rule of God is manifested in the world. [*Ibid.*, pp. 9-10.] Moses was a truly remarkable leader in social action.

In the Ten Commandments the call of God to social action is clearly seen. Sin is revealed here as not just a private transaction between the sinner and God, but as having larger social connotations as well. This is plainly seen in the last six commandments, the second table of the Law: "Honour thy father and thy mother. Thou shalt not kill. Thou shalt not commit adultery. Thou shalt not steal. Thou shalt not bear false witness. Thou shalt not covet" (Exodus 20:12-17).

To the psalmist God's revelation was explicit in this matter of social action. "Trust in the Lord and do good" (Psalms 37:3) is the call made for God's people not only to have faith in Him, but for them to follow up that faith with good works within the community.

The Prophets and Social Action

The prophet Micah declares in the passage that has been called the high water mark of the Old Testament:

> Will the Lord be pleased with thousands of rams, or with ten thousands of rivers of oil? shall I give my firstborn for my transgression, the fruit of my body for the sin of my soul? He hath shewed thee, O man, what is good; and what doth the Lord require of thee, but to do justly, and to love mercy, and to walk humbly with thy God? (Micah 6:7-8).

The prophet's implied answer, when he has asked the question about formal sacrifices, is clearly negative. These things are not what a just and merciful and righteous God required of His people in ancient times, and they are not what He requires of His people today. For what does the Lord require of His people today but to do justly, and to love mercy, and to walk humbly with Him?

In many respects, this is the high point of the Old Testament revelation. There is a sense in which Jesus added nothing to this, but fulfilled it in His person and in His teachings. The ethical message which is largely implicit in the message of Moses and in the Old Testament revelation generally becomes explicit here and elsewhere in the prophets. The social teachings of the prophets supply a degree of concreteness and of social application to specific circumstances which seldom appear elsewhere in the Bible. It is for this reason that the prophets deserve very special attention in any consideration of the Biblical revelation and social action.

The Hebrew prophets were not lone wolves. They emerged from " . . . a religious community and spoke to a religious community . . . . The message of every prophet, Moses, Samuel, Nathan, and Elijah as well as those who came later, was to every individual within the community of Israel, and neither king nor humblest subject was exempt from the obligation to obey the will of Yahweh." [Georgia Harkness, *Christian Ethics* (New York: Abingdon Press, 1957), p. 46.] The prophets were not primarily ethical prophets. They were primarily religious prophets whose vision of God was such that they insisted on right conduct in community. And because they conceived of the Lord God as a God of righteousness, they formed a remarkable body of ideas of how man in community ought to act, what he ought to do in his social relationships.

The burden of the prophetic message was at the point of righteousness and justice and mercy. Their message was an utterly relevant message which was nothing if it was not practical. Jeremiah says, "His word was in mine heart as a burning fire shut up in my bones, and I was weary with forebearing, and I could not stay" (Jeremiah 20:9). And he did not stay. He let his message, the forth-telling that God had called him to do, come out. Amos says, "The lion hath roared, who will not fear? the Lord God hath spoken, who can but prophesy?" (Amos 3:8). And he did prophesy with courage and clarity seldom equalled in the history of the human race.

Concerning this call to righteousness, Walter Rauschenbusch says that the Hebrew prophets "concentrated their incomparable religious energy on the simple demand for righteousness, especially in social and national life. . . . The injustice and the oppression around them seemed intolerable to the prophets, just because the ethical imperative within them was so strong." [*The Social Principles of Jesus* (New York: Association Press, 1927), p. 57.] The prophets succeeded in socializing, or applying to the community, the ideal and the vision of God which they had received. It is a mark of modern religion's degeneracy and essential heresy that this vision of God and His City has become so irrelevant and de-socialized that real sin is not only not denounced but is seldom even recognized.

Justice is another of the burdens of the prophets. Injustice poisoned the community relationships of their day; and injustice, wherever it expresses itself, poisons the relationships within our communities today. It is justice alone which provides the social framework which makes possible the good life for individuals.

The prophets talked a great deal about mercy, about the importance of being merciful and helpful and kind to others, especially to the needy. The prophets were nearly all concerned with the oppression of the poor by the rich.

Norman H. Snaith says that the result of this emphasis has been a linking of the idea of righteousness with the idea of salvation from the very beginning of the prophetic teaching.

> This is a new element which appears for the first time in Amos and his contemporaries. It is one of the most important factors in the development of Old Testament religion, and it makes a fundamental difference between the righteousness of Hebrew religion and the righteousness of Greek ethical writers. With the Greeks, *dikaiosune* (righteousness) has always mainly this reference to conduct. It is an idea of ethical excellence, at its best infused with a goodly humanitarianism. But with the Hebrews, *tsedaqah* (righteousness) had, thanks to the prophets, a fixed and irrevocable association with God's saving activity on behalf of his people.
>
> [Study Notes on Bible Books, Amos, Part I (New York: Abingdon Press, 1945), p. 46. "An Abingdon importation."]

So there is in the Old Testament prophets a marvellous, unique, wonderful emphasis on the connection between salvation and righteousness in community. Complacency about social responsibility and blindness to the significance of community were biases not only of the wealthy but also of the middle classes in the days of the prophets, and they still are today. So the prophets made their emphasis on mercy, and called the people of that day to be helpful toward those who were less fortunate than they. The prophets were interested not only in individuals but also in the entire community to which they spoke. They were concerned about a relevant religion which expressed itself in righteousness, in justice, and in mercy.

The specific messages of the prophets have profound social significance. Consider Elijah's confrontation of Ahab after the murder of Naboth and the confiscation of his vineyard: "Thus saith the Lord, In the place where dogs licked the blood of Naboth shall dogs lick thy blood, even thine" (I Kings 21:19). Elijah, the prophet, in this way strongly defended the ordinary citizen within the community, calling for justice in place of injustice.

Isaiah called the people of God to righteousness with a remarkably well-developed social awareness: "Wash you, make you clean; put away the evil of your doings from before mine eyes; cease to do evil; learn to do well; seek judgment, relieve the oppressed, judge the fatherless, plead for the widow" (Isaiah 1:16-17). Again the Prince of Prophets says: "Woe unto them that join house to house, that lay field to field, until there be no place, that they may be placed alone in the midst of the earth" (Isaiah 5:8).

Jeremiah proclaims a fearless message in calling the people of God to social action:

Thus saith the Lord; Go down to the house of the king of Judah, and speak there this word, and say,

Hear the word of the Lord, O king of Judah, that sittest upon the throne of David, thou, and thy servants, and thy people that enter in by these gates: Thus saith the Lord; Execute ye judgment and righteousness, and deliver the spoiled out of the hand of the oppressor: and do no wrong, do no violence to the stranger, the fatherless, nor the widow, neither shed innocent blood in this place. For if ye do this thing indeed, then shall there enter in by the gates of this house kings sitting upon the throne of David, riding in chariots and on horses, he and his servants, and his people. But if ye will not hear these words, I swear by myself, saith the Lord, that this house shall become a desolation (Jeremiah 22:1-5).

The great Eighth Century prophet, Amos, says, "But let judgment run down as waters, and righteousness as a mighty stream" (Amos 5:24). The general prophetic message concerning social action is well summed up in this word from Amos, and in Micah 6:8. And to that marvelous message of Micah nothing needs to be added save the fulfilling which Christ Jesus accomplished in His life and death and resurrection and the infilling which the Holy Spirit accomplishes in the life of the committed Christian.

Old Testament revelation is remarkably definite in setting out the responsibility God's people have for loving their neighbors. Negatively it is declared, "He that despiseth his neighbour sinneth" (Proverbs 14:21), and positively, "Thou shalt love thy neighbour as thyself" (Leviticus 19:18).

Old Testament revelation is not God's complete revelation. But it is complete enough for God's people to have understood from the beginning their tremendous responsibility to him and to their fellowmen in the area of social concerns and community action.

Jesus and Social Action

The Old Testament in general and the prophets in particular are helpful in providing ethical insights, but it is to Jesus Christ that Christians must go for primary inspiration and strength in today's efforts to make the church effective in social action. Peter declares that Jesus "went about doing good" (Acts 10:38). Jesus Christ Himself was a do-gooder from the beginning of His public ministry to the end of it. There is a sense in which He did nothing else. His death at Calvary was the inevitable climax of such a life of doing good. Through ministry to all the desperate needs of the mass of humanity with whom He came in contact, Jesus manifested the kind of compassionate goodness which an evil world preferred to crucify rather than to crown.

Jesus' platform of community action was well developed but profoundly simple. With marvelous insight He established a platform which is as relevant in the Twentieth Century as it was in the first century:

And he came to Nazareth, where he had been brought up: and, as his custom was, he went into the synagogue on the sabbath day, and stood up for to read. And there was delivered unto him the book of the prophet Esaias. And when he had opened the book, he found the place where it was written, The Spirit of the Lord is upon me, because he hath anointed me to preach the gospel to the poor; he hath sent me to heal the brokenhearted, to preach deliverance to the captives, and recovering

of sight to the blind, to set at liberty them that are
bruised, to preach the acceptable year of the Lord
(Luke 4:16-22).

There is good evidence that social action was considered the proof of Jesus' Messiahship by many in His
own day. It was not enough for Him to be right theologically or right doctrinally in an abstract sense. It was
social action which unmistakably demonstrated His
Messiahship.

> And the disciples of John shewed him of all these
> things. And John calling unto him two of his
> disciples sent them to Jesus, saying, Art thou he
> that should come? or look we for another? When
> then men were come unto him, they said, John
> Baptist hath sent us unto thee, saying, Art thou he
> that should come? or look we for another? And in
> that same hour he cured many of their infirmities
> and plagues, and of evil spirits; and unto many that
> were blind he gave sight. Then Jesus answering
> said unto them, Go your way, and tell John what
> things ye have seen and heard; how that the blind
> see, the lame walk, the lepers are cleansed, the
> deaf hear, the dead are raised, to the poor the
> gospel is preached. And blessed is he, whosoever
> shall not be offended in me (Luke 7:18-23).

There are also indications in the life and ministry of
Jesus Christ that social action is the final test of true
religion. The witness of Jesus is:

> When the Son of man shall come in his glory, and
> all the holy angels with him, then shall he sit upon

the throne of his glory: and before him shall be
gathered all nations: and he shall separate them
one from another, as a shepherd divideth his sheep
from the goats: and he shall set the sheep on his
right hand, but the goats on the left. Then shall the
King say unto them on his right hand, Come, ye
blessed of my Father, inherit the kingdom prepared for you from the foundation of the world:
for I was an hungered, and ye gave me meat: I was
thirsty, and ye gave me drink: I was a stranger,
and ye took me in: naked, and ye clothed me: I
was sick, and ye visited me: I was in prison, and
ye came unto me. Then shall the righteous answer
him, saying, Lord, when saw we thee an hungered,
and fed thee? or thirsty, and gave thee drink?
When saw we thee a stranger, and took thee in?
or naked, and clothed thee? Or when saw we thee
sick, or in prison, and came unto thee? And the
King shall answer and say unto them, Verily I say
unto you, Inasmuch as ye have done it unto one of
the least of these my brethren, ye have done it
unto me (Matthew 25:31-46).

And He went on to say immediately that if they had
not done these things to the least of these within the
community, they had failed to do them unto Him. At
the heart of God Himself is social action, work among
human beings, helpful service to persons in need
wherever they may be found.

The Beatitudes in particular and the Sermon on the
Mount in general must be considered for there is deep
concern here for social action.

Some prominent Christians have insisted that the
Sermon on the Mount is intended for another dispensa-

tion, that it was never meant for this world, and that it is better to ignore it as far as the hard realities of daily life are concerned. Even a casual reading of this tremendous statement reveals, however, that its message is not intended for another world. Though these ideals cannot be given fullness of expression in this kind of a sin-cursed world, this is the very place where they are desperately needed. Social action of this kind will not be needed in the world to come, but it is sorely needed in this present world.

The method of social action approved by Jesus is given in His parable of kingdom growth, in Luke 13: 20-21. These two verses contain one of the shortest of all the parables, but they help us to understand that the kingdom comes powerfully and pervasively.

> And again he said, Whereunto shall I liken the kingdom of God? It is like leaven, which a woman took and hid in three measures of meal, till the whole was leavened.

How are Christians to get involved in community action? The involvement is like leaven in a lump; not with revolutionary violence, not with the expectation that in a day we can bring in the kingdom. All of those who have worked at it very long have seen already that this cannot be done. The fact is, however, that God wants his people to be laboring, working, ministering, serving, and doing, as leaven in the lump, moving steadily toward the goal which God has in mind for mankind.

An idea of social action is given even in the familiar passage commonly called the Great Commission.

> Go ye therefore, and teach all nations, baptizing
> them in the name of the Father, and of the Son,
> and of the Holy Ghost: teaching them to observe
> all things whatsoever I have commanded you: and,
> lo, I am with you alway, even unto the end of the
> world (Matthew 28:19-20).

The teaching of His disciples to observe all things
that Christ has commanded is a carrying into the community of His full gospel. The task of world evangeliza-
tion, of global missions, to which Jesus assigned His
disciples, is a task of extending the blessed community
of Christ Jesus until "the kingdoms of this world are
become the kingdoms of our Lord, and of his Christ."
Jesus never meant this "Go ye into all the world, and
preach the gospel" as a narrow command to go to distant places and to recruit neophytes into the ranks of
the initiated. This, from the beginning, was a charge for
believers to confront the whole person in the whole
world with the whole Christ. This is still His mandate
to Christians today: to confront the whole person in the
whole community—and ultimately in the whole world—
with the whole Christ, who has the power "to save to
the uttermost them that come to God by him."

Jesus, the Lord, died on a cross made up of two
pieces: a vertical piece to stand in some way for man's
right relationship to God, and a horizontal piece to
stand in some way for man's right relationship to His
fellow men. And Jesus was not teaching His disciples
just a little bit of pretty ritual when He taught them to
pray, "Thy kingdom come. Thy will be done in earth,
as it is in heaven." On the contrary, this is a vital, significant, and definite part of Christ's wonderful gospel.

The New Testament Churches and Social Action

The New Testament churches did not project themselves into community life to any great extent. They
could not have done so and lived. They had an obligation, a stewardship, a duty, to survive. "The New
Testament is written throughout with a terrible earnest-
ness, by men who believed that the end of the world
was close at hand." [E. F. Scott, *Man and Society in the
New Testament* (New York: Charles Scribner's Sons,
1946), p. vii.] The New Testament churches did not
have any special love or esteem for the world or for
the institutions of their communities. They faced the
world and its institutions with a mixture of contempt,
submission, and relative recognition. These they felt
were provisional arrangements that had to be endured
until Jesus came again. Still, it is very important to
understand that the New Testament churches did not
so despair of society in general and of their various
communities in particular that they completely with-
drew their seasoning from it and made of the church a
monastic mountain of savorless salt.

Perhaps it will be helpful to consider the characteristics of the early churches as they involved themselves
in social action. The New Testament churches were
often in conflict with their communities. By their nature, they set themselves in sharp, clear opposition to
oppressive and damaging ways of life. These New
Testament churches were cradled in conflict with their
communities. They grew up in conflict, and like Christ
the Lord, won many of their most significant triumphs
by a calm but determined defiance of particular evils
that brought crucifixion as a prelude to resurrection.

While the New Testament churches were often in

conflict with the world around them, they were persistent in their devotion to righteousness. The early churches went underground in some respects, resorting to symbols and codes and apocalypses to communicate with one another. Yet they kept right on striking their blows for righteousness, for justice, for truth, and for freedom. They, of all people, were not sitting back and doing nothing. For them the chief end of man was not to get peace of mind and enjoy it forever. [Cf. John H. Marion's chapter entitled "The Christian and Community Conflicts," Malcolm P. Calhoun, *Christians Are Citizens* (Richmond: John Knox Press, 1957), pp. 66-100.] Their purpose in life was to be so true to Christ in every area and relationship of life that ultimately the cursed community would be transformed into the blessed community.

The New Testament churches did not try to avoid decisions in their relationship to society in their day. Christians ought not to do so today. They were persistent in devotion to righteousness. Christians ought to be persistent and faithful in devotion to righteousness today. Karl Barth says at this point that the church today must

> . . . look and see whether she is not now really, of necessity, compromising herself, i.e. compromising herself with the Devil, to whom no ally is dearer than a Church, so absorbed in caring for her good reputation and clean garments, that she keep eternal silence, is eternally meditating, eternally discussing, eternally neutral; a church so troubled about the transcendence of the Kingdom of God—a thing which isn't really so easy to menace!—that she has become a dumb dog. This is just the thing

that must not take place—must not take place
today. [From *The Church and the Political Prob-
lems of Our Day*, by Karl Barth, p. 21, Charles
Scribner's Sons. Quoted by Holmes Rolston, *The
Social Message of The Apostle Paul* (Richmond:
John Knox Press, 1942), p. 79.]

The great theologian is here calling today's churches to
the same sort of thing that the churches of the New
Testament era committed themselves to: persistence
in devotion to practical righteousness in every area and
relationship of life.

Again, the New Testament churches were faithful in
spite of opposition. The early Christians were admonished to endure suffering for Christ's sake. As John
Marion has pointed out,

> These folk had no particular scorn for popularity
> and no distaste for wealth and prestige if in good
> conscience those things could be acquired; they
> were just convinced that some other values were
> always more important. They had no relish for
> being called bad names; they simply had a vital
> concern for Christianity's good name, a concern so
> strong that any bad names they might be called
> became inconsequential. In the words of Edmund
> Burke's tribute to a British statesman for his fight
> against the tyranny of the East India Company,
> they "put to hazard" their ease, their security, and
> their popularity, knowing that for the Christian
> citizen no less than for effective public servants
> anywhere, "calumny and abuse are essential parts
> of triumph." [Op. cit., p. 93.]

Most of the early Christians were faithful in spite of opposition. They were deeply convinced that it was better for them to lose their shirts than for them to lose their souls.

The New Testament churches were also marked by courageous idealism. Their witness was distinguished not by caution calculated to protect their peace, but by a courage calculated to project their principles. The New Testament Christians permeated their communities not with the deliberate and direct revolutionary intent of breaking down and destroying evil institutions within the communities and then inaugurating new ones, but with vigorous new ideas, higher ideals, a superior mind, and a better way of life. If Christians do the same for today's communities, it will be not so much with programs as with vigorous ideas, a better way of life, and higher ideals than those subscribed to by the world about us.

The New Testament churches did not have specific programs of social reform in their community action, but they did have Christ and the gospel so that social reform in the community inevitably came, and with awful and positive power. The Christian gospel is still the most powerful force on earth for social reform and human betterment. But Christian witness is authenticated only as it is actualized in the definite choices of life, in definite decisions which relate to all the multitude of contemporary questions which trouble the world and agitate the churches. So, while Christians believe that the real answer to all community problems is Christ and the gospel, it is understood that the way the gospel becomes truly good news and the way Christ becomes a living Saviour to needy persons is for believers to express His will in social action. The New

Testament churches, in the power of God, set in motion the processes which are destroying those things in society that are out of harmony with the holy purposes of God for the life of man.

The message of the New Testament churches contained both radical and conservative elements. The New Testament churches had a conservative attitude toward political and social life, but they had a radical attitude toward individual spiritual renewal, the development of religious personality, and the fellowship of such personalities among themselves. It is this radical principle of early Christianity which called in question all the orders of society in general and of these various communities in particular. Ernst Troeltsch has pointed out that these conservative and radical attitudes which are apparently diametrically opposed to each other are not really two equally possible applications existing side by side. They really belong to each other and are united in the fundamental idea of Christianity from which they sprang. [*The Social Teaching of the Christian Churches* (London: George Allen and Unwin, Ltd., 1931, 1949), Vol. I, pp. 82-86.] This concept is particularly seen in the prophets, who brought salvation and works vitally and positively together.

Paul consistently proclaims both the radical and conservative principles. With regard to the sexes, he says radically that in Christ there is neither male nor female, and conservatively that wives must be subject to their husbands and that women must keep silence in the church. With regard to slavery, he says radically that in Christ there is neither bond nor free, and conservatively that slaves should be content with their station in life. With regard to the state, he says conservatively that the powers that be are ordained of God, but radically he projects the principles that involved the churches within a few years in a life and death struggle with emperor worship. By the balancing of these radical and conservative principles, Paul is saved on the one hand from absurdity of proclaiming an absolute ethic in a sinful world and on the other hand from proclaiming an other-worldly religion that would become an opiate to the people as it offered "pie in the sky by and by." While Christians today should not proclaim an absolute ethic in a sinful world, the main interest of the church has always been on the side of the radical ideal, and the main weight of the church must always be thrown in the direction of this ideal.

The general attitude of the New Testament churches to the communities in which they lived swayed between the two extremes of separation on the one hand and association on the other. The monastic tendency, or the tendency toward seclusion, was nurtured by the obvious fact that the world was unsympathetic and hostile, full of sin and evil (such as the requirement of emperor worship and the persecution of Christians), and that by association with it Christians might be defiled. Christians were admonished to separate themselves from the world, Babylon: "Come out of her, my people, lest you take part in her sins, lest you share in her plagues" (Revelation 8:4 RSV). This is an evidence of the monastic tendency, a tendency toward withdrawal and separation. Still, the tendency toward association with the community at large was nurtured by the desire of the believers to exert a Christian influence within the community on individuals and on society and its institutions, by the desire to live such an exemplary life that no reproach should ever be cast on the Name that they know to be above every name.

Paul is the major source of our knowledge of the way in which New Testament churches adjusted themselves to the lives of the communities in which they lived. His concern with social action is seen particularly in Galatians 6:10, where he says: "As we have therefore opportunity, let us do good unto all men, especially unto them who are of the household of faith." Another example of his commitment to social action is seen in his exhortation to the Thessalonians, "And we exhort you, brethren, admonish the idle, encourage the fainthearted, help the weak, be patient with them all. See that none of you repays evil for evil, but always seek to do good to one another and to all" (I Thessalonians 5:14-15 RSV).

Paul generally divides his epistles into two very definite divisions, with the theoretical or the doctrinal matters coming first, and then the practical expression coming last as the climax to his epistles. This method is seen especially in Romans, Ephesians, Galatians, and Colossians. For instance, in Romans he spends the first 11 chapters dealing with the fundamental doctrines of the Christian faith; and then he comes to the doctrine of social action, which forms the natural superstructure for the foundation he has been laying: "I beseech you therefore, brethren, by the mercies of God, that ye present your bodies a living sacrifice, holy, acceptable unto God, which is your reasonable service. And be not conformed to this world: but be ye transformed by the renewing of your mind that you may prove what is that good, and acceptable, and perfect, will of God." (Romans 12:1-2). Then the apostle goes on to talk about citizenship, and paying debts, and various kinds of social action.

The New Testament churches were in the community, part and parcel of the community, but never satisfied with it. They called on men to repent and to prepare themselves for the blessed community which is always in the process of becoming. They were in constant tension with the community that was, and in constant expectancy of the community that should be. They sought to bring the redemptive power of the gospel of Christ to every individual in the community, but they also sought to transform the community's social institutions so as to make them fit instruments for the use of redeemed men and women. [Cf. Tilford T. Swearingen, *The Community and Christian Education* (St. Louis: Bethany Press, 1950), p. 57. Quoted by Albert Terrill Rasmussen, *Christian Social Ethics* (Englewood Cliffs, N. J.: Prentice-Hall., 1956), p. 201.]

Surely the task of Christians today can be no less than to apply within the whole context of society the full gospel of this same, wonderful Lord.

CHAPTER 3

The Church and the World

"I hate, I despise your feasts, and I take no delight in your solemn assemblies. Even though you offer me your burnt offerings and cereal offerings, I will not accept them, and the peace offerings of your fatted beasts I will not look upon. Take away from me the noise of your songs; to the melody of your harps I will not listen. But let justice roll down like waters, and righteousness like an overflowing stream" Amos 5:21-24 (RSV).

The word of Amos could hardly be more piercingly, startlingly relevant than it is to the contemporary churchman's situation. We have a name that we are living, but there are some ugly clouds on the horizon that indicate we may be dead. We assure ourselves that we are fully clothed but we have a haunting suspicion that we are actually naked. We marshal an impressive array of statistics to prove that we are succeeding, but we harbor a lingering fear that we are really failing. We firmly believe that we are free but we keep running blindly and bruisingly into walls that we are positive are not supposed to be there. We keep shouting from the housetops that we are, too, overwhelmingly committed to evangelism, missions, and stewardship, but deep down inside there dwells a haunting fear that, like the Ephesians, we have, in fact, missed getting acquainted with the Holy Spirit.

The situation is serious. It calls for frankness, candor, courage, and vision. May God help His people to have eyes to see and ears to hear today what His Spirit is saying to the churches.

I. Evidences of the World in the Church

Among the evidences of the world in the church, there are four which deserve special attention in this context: a reflection of the culture, a frenzied institutionalism, a burgeoning bureaucracy, and a willingness to be used.

1. Reflection of the Culture

Most denominational groups on the American scene today accurately, even slavishly, reflect the culture of which they are a part. Churchmen generally find the vain traditions of men a great deal more palatable than the clear teachings of the New Testament, in spite of all our solemn genuflections in the direction of loyalty to the word of God.

Through the years, much of the church has demonstrated a consistent refusal, unwillingness, or inability, to be prophetic. We have simply been too closely identified with our respective cultures to raise our voices for God against them and the evils they condone, foster, nurture, and support.

The culture is materialistic. The churches have a way

of reflecting this materialism. We lionize anybody who being rich will stay with us.

We orient ourselves to success. Americans generally must succeed or perish. The churches often indicate that we are concerned with succeeding first and walking humbly with God afterward. Success we measure by budgets, salaries, baptisms, new buildings, gifts to missions, pastor's homes, advances in position, rank, or place of service. Much of the present harried soul-searching about the slow-down of our Sunday School growth, rate of baptisms, and development of stewardship gives the appearance of being concerned more with getting the assembly line to rolling again than with getting on with the work of Jesus Christ, our Savior and Lord.

The culture, moreover, is neatly, tightly organized. It has, in due time, come to pass that the churches have decided we must be organized or perish. While there is ample justification for seeking more efficient methods of organization for our growing work, it is now fairly obvious that the organizational jag which the churches have now been on for about two decades has gone a good deal further than was originally intended. We are discovering that the camel's nose is followed in due time by atrocious humps. Organization undoubtedly serves a fine purpose not only in assembling, distributing, and selling automobiles but also in teaching the Bible and in training for church membership. That it is not an unmixed blessing in churches and in church boards, agencies, and conventions, can be demonstrated by anyone with a concern for human values who will talk with some of the people directly involved in this new organizational revolution, or who will go to the trouble to analyze the new polarization of power which takes place in the wake of the recommendations of the organization experts. In thus borrowing from the organizational techniques of big business, we again give evidence of our inter-relatedness with the culture. The present high pitch of organizational concern is by no means new. For at least fifty years there has been a popularly accepted idea written large in American church life to the effect that cooperation is a test of fellowship. The step from cooperation, which someone must originate and promote, to finely honed organization is a natural, if not inevitable one, which the churches have now taken in due course.

As the culture is activistic, so American church life has grown to be increasingly activistic. An almost unbelievable multiplication of committee meetings now plague the projection of any meaningful ministry in either the local church or in the denominations. One of the appalling things about this activism is that we never have time to stop and catch that vision of God without which any people will surely perish. The activism which the churches are now reflecting also carries with it the added disadvantage of effectively smothering creativity. This means, of course, that unless we can check our present activism, we will more and more turn in on ourselves rather than find new ways of validating our Christian insights and principles in the new world opening before us.

2. *Frenzied Institutionalism*

Another evidence of the world in the church is the frenzied institutionalism which marks the Christian movement on many fronts. This institutionalism may well be prompted by the fear that the church's power and glory are slipping and that we must build boxes in which to keep these qualities lest we lose them entirely. The time was when the verbalized motto of most foreign mission societies was, "Institutionalize or Die." The policy still generally prevails. So while Communists are sending one man or a half dozen operatives into key spots like a national university to touch the lives of literally hundreds of tomorrow's key leaders, the churches have pursued a policy of building huge brick buildings to house institutional programs even if this approach clearly and abysmally fails to produce spiritually acceptable results.

Our institutionalism is to be seen not only in our local churches and in our foreign mission programs but also in our colleges, our childrens' homes, our homes for the aging, our bent to building, our edifices and "sanctuaries," our boards, bureaus, committees, and our parochial schools.

The parochial school idea deserves attention for it may possibly be the tragic wave of the future for American churches. There is reason to fear that this Christian school idea may catch hold and begin to spread like wildfire. Most of the churches have the educational facilities in which to house parochial schools. The argument is increasingly and tellingly being made that there is no rational argument *against* Christian parochial schools from grades one through twelve and *for* them for grades thirteen through sixteen. If Ernst Troeltsch's theory is right that the really seminal ideas and the genuinely creative work in religion is done by the lower classes, then we may expect that some of the present activity for parochial schools at the lowest levels of the church's grass roots will be picked up, polished, and refined by more sophisticated churches. Such forces as are represented by the vested interests of already existing denominational colleges and the as yet unmeasured commitment to the principle of separation of church and state may be expected to oppose the proliferation of Christian parochial schools. Our present preoccupation with institutionalism, however, keeps one from being over-confident in the face of this threat.

What can the free churches do with their institutionalism? They can give up their radical freedom or they can give up their institutionalism. They cannot have both. No consequential organized group in history, however, has ever voluntarily given up its institutions and its institutional programs. None probably could have done so and lived. It is clear that the radical freedom which many American churches have wistfully clung to is going. Perhaps it has, in fact, already gone. One of the most important questions facing Christians today is the evolving of a satisfactory integration of Christian freedom on the one hand and Christian institutionalism on the other. Institutionalism is an impressive instrument but a grossly inadequate god.

3. Burgeoning Bureaucracy

While there has been valiant opposition to the proliferation of church bureaus, it has been largely ineffective. The statistics indicate that this is true not only on a state and national level, in the various church institutions, and in the denominational boards and agencies, but also in the local churches. The bureaucracy is a dragon that can be argued against, but we have yet to produce a knight in shining armor who can slay it. Indeed, we find it absolutely necessary for the doing of the various tasks we have assumed. Yet the bureaucracy is another indication that the world is in the church.

4. *Willingness to Be Used*

The only other evidence of the world in the church to which there is time to give attention in this context is our willingness to be used. This willingness to be used, this neurotic prostitution of ourselves, shows up in numerous ways. Some of the nation's best known church leaders have their pictures displayed in double-page spreads advertising insurance policies. Many pulpits during recent elections have sounded ominously like one political party or the other gathered for prayer. It is curious that the great, and important, principle of separation of church and state has received practically no pulpit attention since November of 1960 from those voices that were so articulate prior to the election! Moreover, there are numerous indications that both the national and the state governments are more and more looking on the churches as another of their numerous natural resources. While this attitude may be both natural and inevitable for the governments, it is a tragic phenomenon to see the churches playing along in this deadly game. If they do not maintain their freedom, they cannot maintain their usefulness either to the Kingdom of God or the kingdoms of men.

All of this willingness to be used suggests that at least many church leaders are lacking in that single-minded commitment to God and concern with the doing of His will without which we shall surely be tossed about by every wind of doctrine.

The world is indeed, and to our mutual dismay, in the church.

And what is to be said about the church in the world?

II. A Look at the Church in the World

It is painfully obvious that the world today pays the

church very little mind. Churchmen now and then yap at the world's heels, but it really couldn't care less. We still go through the motions of being opposed to alcohol but the world has discovered that we no longer pack any punch. The roaring lion has become a very tame house cat. The mighty stream has dwindled to a timid trickle. The rushing wind has calmed to become a gentle zephyr. The modern world neither experiences our naked power nor encounters the thrust of our moral strength, as it did when Christians were, though despised and rejected, still sure of the rightness of their cause.

In our present condition the churches seem to find getting in gear so as to keep from being effectively segregated from the real forces of power in our world either undesirable or impossible. There is a growing polarization of opinion that it is really undesirable to get in and "mix it" with the world. The world is doomed, the reasoning goes, we have not long to suffer its abuse, we have no mandate to change it and the best thing for us to do is to withdraw from it as quickly and completely as possible. Others, however, would genuinely like to get in gear, to speak for God to the world, to bear our witness in some meaningful way where the big decisions are being made, to translate God's word into a language that can be understood in the workaday world. The sad fact, however, is that we have not yet found the ways to do it. For the churches to become merely another power bloc is something which most of us are unwilling to do in the light of Christian insights and convictions. For us to get involved in direct efforts to try to influence specific national policies about Viet Nam or Rhodesia does not strike us as being generally either desirable or effective. And yet to continue, as we have been doing, to get our satisfaction out of simply electing a Baptist governor, a Methodist congressman, or a Presbyterian president is proving to be a pretty shallow and empty way for the church to get its "kicks."

Our condition as far as an effective influencing of the big decisions in the community, the state, the nation, or the world is extremely weak.

The loss of spiritual thrust in our work is another factor to be considered in this look at the condition of the church in the world. There is a certain barrenness in our worship that all of our talk, seminary courses, plans, meetings, speeches, and denominational emphases cannot hide for we have no clear vision of God.

There is a certain woodenness in our missions that all of our rallies, offerings, and lip service to the missions cause cannot quite cover up for we have a sneaking suspicion that our flag of missions is really flying at half-mast.

There is a certain sterility about our evangelism which all of our talk, articles, books, conferences, and ritualistic blood-letting does not conceal for we feel that the real concern is not for people but for attendance, additions, money, results.

There is a certain soullessness in our stewardship which all of our big-business promotional schemes, hard-sell techniques, and harsh, high pressuring cannot obliterate for there smolders among us a bitter resentment of stewardship rather than a glad, exuberant, hilarious desire to give freely in view of the fact that from God in Christ we have freely received.

There is, moreover, a certain preoccupation with "image" among us which indicates we are not so concerned about who and what we really are before God almighty as we are about what people think of us.

The condition of the church in the world is that the old formulae no longer produce results, the artificial stimuli no longer evoke a response. The bright fires of yesterday are turning to ashes at just the time when it is most important for them to burn with unprecedented brilliance.

III. A Presumption of a Prescription

Is there no balm in Gilead? Must Toynbee have been the last word? Shall we now sit down and plan the funeral service for the church? Shall we say, "Dust to dust, ashes to ashes," and throw the clods down on the coffin as has been suggested by a score of ecclesiastical diagnosticians? Are we to make Job's friends and Lot's wife our heroes because they sang our song?

No. The church is not doomed. It is now necessary for us to face frankly these issues, however, for no good could possibly come from thrusting our heads deeper into the sand. To pretend we have no problems is as defeating an error in the long run as to believe we have nothing but problems.

The church today has many strengths. Church membership is at an all-time high. Participation in church programs and ministries is extremely gratifying. More people are actually being evangelized and baptized annually than ever before in the history of the Christian movement. Modern churches have a good program for the education of ministers. We have a superior program of religious education, if you measure it by what the churches have done down through history. We have a very lively interest in, and commitment to, the concept of world missions. The evangelical churches still have a strong hold on such insights as the priesthood of the believer, the worth of the individual, and the significance of freedom which the world desperately needs and which God wants maintained. There are some heartening signs of renewed spiritual vigor in the liturgical churches. The church does have its strong points.

But let us not be blinded by these strengths to the weaknesses which we must correct lest we sicken and die.

What can we do? We can with the help of God, begin to make those decisions and do that work which will move us outward, into the world, rather than inward, away from it.

The church must encourage, promote, magnify, and emphasize individual encounter with God. Walter Rauschenbusch, in a remarkable statement entitled "Why I Am a Baptist" says, "The Christian faith as Baptists hold it sets spiritual experience boldly to the front as the one great thing in religion . . . . The more I study the history of religion, the more I see how great and fruitful such a position is." [Sydnor Stealey, *A Baptist Treasury* (New York: Thomas Y. Crowell Company, 1958), pp. 166, 169.] While all Christians make a place for some kind of emphasis on experience, there is critical need now for special attention to this matter. Through our preaching, teaching, writing, and promoting we as Christians communicate our understanding of this great and fruitful position—that because of Christ lost man can encounter God and be saved. This encounter, people generally must be led to understand, is not just a psychological experience in which the soul is saved. Among most evangelical Christians the emphasis has too long been laid on the psychological aspects of the gospel in new birth to the exclusion of an emphasis on continuing encounter with God, which encounter results in the building of Christian character.

There is one pastor of whom a fellow preacher said, after he had hastily departed to another state in a blaze of evangelistic glory, "He loved souls but he hated people." To experience the grace of God is not simply to have a theoretical transaction to take place within that shadowy substance that preachers call the soul. It is to receive from God medicine for our sickness, a covering for our nakedness, a continuing shelter of love and acceptance. A vast multitude of church members generally think of salvation as something they *had* rather than as something they *have*. That is, they conceive it as past and future rather than as past, *present*, and future. Today's churches can experience the blessings of God's renewal only as they inject the element of this *present* into our general thought in life.

The knowledge that the churches are no longer as independent and radically free as they once were ought not to discourage modern Christians from joining in a concerted effort to formulate and give expression to a responsible freedom. Such an effort will certainly require more intelligent, even brilliant, *communication* than we have experienced in recent decades between church members and the world. It will require sacrificial labor to translate the Word of God into a language all men can understand. It may involve less golf, less boating, less television, less fellowship, less sleep, less cowardice, less committee activism, even less preaching. It may require an evolutionary shedding or perhaps a traumatic cutting off of those institutions and institutional programs which we determine are at once destroying our freedom, sapping our strength, and separating us from our Christian calling.

In Anton Chekov's "Cherry Orchard," Anya says to her weeping mother when the news is broken of the sale of their ancestral home, "Don't weep, mamma. We will make a new garden, more splendid than this one; and you will see it, you will understand. And joy, quiet, deep joy, will sink into your soul like the sun at evening! And you will smile, mamma!" [*The Plays of Chekhov,* Modern Library (New York: Random House), p. 104.] If we must cut off some of our present institutionalism with its extension of programs, organizations, bureaus, meetings, drives, and goals, then let us do so with courage and dispatch.

Responsible freedom is not a goal which we can easily come by; but it is one worthy of diligent pursual.

If we really are to become the "New Testament Churches" that we keep telling ourselves we already are, there must be a complete acceptance of the relevance of Christianity to daily life. Through theological education, Bible teaching, regular preaching, and denominational programming there must be a communication to the world of the concept that Christianity is not just a batch of hocus-pocus; that Christ's life is not only vicarious but also exemplary; that our faith is not only historical but also contemporary.

Those who occupy places of leadership in the church must decide whether we prefer being hated by the ignorant if we speak out or being despised by the wise if we are silent. We must determine whether we want to be hounded by hell for assuming the redemptive role of the Christian or be alienated from heaven for neglecting the weightier matters of the law. We must make our choice as to whether we want to give ourselves to a vain effort to escape from the world or to bear our cross of self-sacrifice daily in the world.

How can the church bear its cross daily? How can we "mix it" with the world? How can we get in gear?

Not by hiring lobbyists. Not by becoming a pressure group, speaking for so many hundred churches or so many million Christians. Not by copying the methods for engaging the gears now being used by the various lobbies.

We must rather get in gear as the early Christians did, by moral integrity, by practical righteousness, by Christian character, by consistent holiness, by personal honor, and by uncompromised commitment to Christ's Lordship in every area and relationship of life. And we must do all this, not separately, but together. The finding of ways to bear our witness for Christ together is surely one of the greatest tasks of these times.

There is not a minute to waste in geting the world out of the church and the church into the world.

CHAPTER 4

A Christian Looks at the Communist Threat

The Communist Manifesto begins with the words: "A spectre is haunting Europe—the spectre of communism." After one hundred years the spectre is haunting not only Europe but the entire world with a vengeance born in hell.

The communist movement has now gained control of one-fourth of the earth's land area and one-third of the world's people. Almost a billion people, including the citizens of Red China and Soviet Russia, which are the first and third most populous nations on earth, now live under communist domination. In the past fifty years communism has been gaining territory and converts at a faster rate than any political or religious movement in history.

In the free world today a great many books, articles, pamphlets, films, programs, and organizations have mushroomed to meet the demand for information on communism. It has finally dawned on us that here is a subject which non-communists cannot remain ignorant of and still survive as free men. Communism is obviously an evil force with awesome power which must be reckoned with. It will not be ignored. Its influence in international affairs cannot be denied. Its threat to world peace is without doubt real. Its menace to the institutions of society is in many respects the most serious and vicious in the history of mankind. Its antagonism to Christianity is of such depth and breadth and height as has never before been experienced by Christians.

Abraham Lincoln once said, "If we could first know where we are and whither we are tending we could better know what to do and how to do it." There is obviously a need for this kind of knowledge of communism today. An effort is being made to meet that need by such a varied array of organizations and individuals as the Pentagon, the United States Chamber of Commerce, the Federal Bureau of Investigation, J. Edgar Hoover, the American Legion, the John Birch Society, a small army of affluently retired army brass, sundry evangelists, organized labor, the National Association of Manufacturers, almost all the churches and denominations, and even Hugh Hefner. Hefner, editor of *Playboy* magazine and "czar of the bunny empire" that includes a nationwide chain of nightclubs dedicated to the exploitation of a sophomoric weakness in American males who are willing to pay generously to see female nudity, would have us believe that his formula somehow is in the forefront of the fight against communism—of all things—and for the American way of life.

There is a very real sense in which the United States of America as a nation must concern itself with the communist threat for the designs for world conquest by the USSR are abundantly evident. All citizens have a stake in this concern.

There is an extraordinary sense, however, in which Christian citizens must concern themselves with communism for the communists are irrevocably dedicated to the destruction of religion in general and to the obliteration of Christianity in particular.

The editor of *Paixe and Liberte*, a French communist newspaper, wrote in 1954: "The Gospel is a much more powerful weapon for the renewal of society than is our Marxist philosophy. All the same, it is we who will finally beat you. We are only a handful, and you Christians are numbered by the millions. But if you remember the story of Gideon and his three hundred companions you will understand why I am right. We Communists do not play with words. We are realists, and seeing that we are determined to achieve our object, we know how to obtain the means. Of our salaries and wages we keep only what is strictly necessary; and we give the rest for propaganda purposes. To this propaganda we also consecrate all our free time and part of our holidays. You, however, give only a little time and hardly any money for the spreading of the Gospel of Christ. How can anyone believe in the supreme value of this Gospel if you do not practice it? If you do not spread it? And if you sacrifice neither time nor money for it? Believe me, it is we who will win, for we believe in our Communist message and we are ready to sacrifice everything, even our life, in order that social justice shall triumph. But you people are afraid to soil your hands." [Quoted by Robert H. Spiro, Jr. in a pamphlet entitled "Christianity and Communism" in *Blue Ridge Bulletin*, Vol. 23, July 1959, No. 3, Black Mountain, N.C., p. 7 (unnumbered).]

It is axiomatic that hard problems have no easy solutions. Those who offer a simple and painless panacea for communism are either ignorant or charlatans or ignorant charlatans.

Let us here seek to penetrate the heavy fog of emotionalism that surrounds much of the current talk about communism and try to come to a better understanding of the foe we face. What is this thing of communism which Churchill called "a riddle wrapped up in an enigma inside a mystery"? Who is the foe we face?

The History of Communism

The word "communism" was coined in the secret revolutionary societies of Paris in the 1830s. The word originally referred to the common ownership and use of property and represented an ancient ideal of a society free from injustice. Karl Marx (1818-1883) and Frederich Engels (1820-1895) working together formulated the basic doctrines of what they called "scientific socialism." It is fundamentally their doctrine which today is called communism. They stated communism's basic aims in the *Communist Manifesto,* written in 1848, and in *Capital,* the first volume of which was printed in 1867. It was really Karl Marx with his overwhelmingly single-minded discipline and his tremendous drive who gave vision, direction, and purpose to the communist movement. Engels clarified and popularized the ponderous and often obscure writing of Marx. Lenin further expanded the body of communist ideas and principles during the quarter century prior to his death in 1924.

Lenin was more responsible than any other man for leading the first successful revolutionary Communist Party and he was the real founder of the Soviet state in Russia. It is Lenin's USSR which today still embodies pre-eminence, authority, and power in the communist world, in spite of China's vigorous challenge of that authority. The Communist Party in the USSR, with only about eight million members, has the Russian government under its absolute control. From the headquarters in Moscow, and from the would-be headquarters in Peking, the whole communist world gets its signals; and from those two headquarters there is being directed continuing campaigns to spread the doctrine of communism to the uttermost part of the earth.

The doctrine of communal ownership founded on the abolition of private property has probably had adherents of one kind or another throughout human history and particularly for the past two thousand years.

Common ownership of material things has always held an appeal to certain groups within the Christian community. The experience of the Jerusalem church in its experiment with community of goods is recorded in the fourth chapter of Acts:

> "And the multitude of them that believed were of one heart and one soul: neither said any of them that ought of the things which he possessed was his own; but they had all things in common. And with great power gave the apostles witness of the resurrection of the Lord Jesus: and great grace was upon them all. Neither was there any among them that lacked: for as many as were possessors of lands or houses sold them, and brought the prices of the things that were sold, and laid them down at the apostles' feet: and distribution was made unto every man according as he had need" (Acts 4:32-35).

Such groups as the Hutterite brethren and the Bruderhof and Koinonia fellowships still practice community of goods on distinctively Christian grounds.

Karl Marx was undoubtedly familiar with the early theories about, and experiments with, communism. It is impossible to determine whether he derived his own doctrine of communal ownership of property from the writings of Mably, from some German account of French communism, or from some unknown source in his prodigious reading and interminable dialogue with other revolutionaries. At any rate, he became thoroughly convinced of the validity of the doctrine of common ownership of property and it became a key plank in his platform.

The experiment of the early Christians with communism may well have been their attempt to rise personally above concern for material things and to help, in a spirit of genuine Christian love, those within their fellowship who were in need. The experiments of the idealistic humanists and the vigorously dogmatic rationalists of the mid-nineteenth century were attempts to bring order and justice to a social system that was all too clearly chaotic and unjust.

The social conditions of the Nineteenth Century which gave rise to communism deserve some attention in our consideration of communism's history. During the most formative years of Karl Marx, the social chaos engendered by the burgeoning industrial revolution was almost unbelievably bad. He saw the wretched slums, the child labor, the crowded hovels, the merciless exploitation of workers, and all the other grim realities of everyday life in the crudest years of the industrial revolution. It is impossible to familiarize one's self with the life and work of Karl Marx and these social conditions without seeing the connection between the two. John K. Jessup says in his article, "The Story of Marxism: Its Men, Its March" that "socialism" was a word of great power in nineteenth century Europe "because the industrial revolution struck that unlucky continent before democracy did. Not until after 1890 did working men win the vote in Belgium and Sweden, for example, and then only by means of Socialist led general strikes. The Socialist cause, in the 1840's, carried the torch, not only for the new factory-working class but for basic political rights and civil liberties, which Americans had won sixty years before." (*Life*, October 20, 1961, p. 111.)

The last quarter of the Nineteenth Century was a period of waiting and floundering for the communist movement. The creative work had already been done. The worst abuses of the industrial revolution began gradually to be corrected. The first violent thrust of revolutionary zeal both among the workers and among the intelligentsia began to run its course. The intellectual and political turmoil which had so long marked Europe began to be abated.

If it had not been for Russia, the world almost certainly would have no communist problem today. One authority on communism says that if the movement had been confined to the West it would have done much good and little harm. But it was not confined to the West. It became a Western heresy. It went to Russia and in that vast country with its complex culture it was transformed into a monstrous Frankenstein. It became a distorted form of Marxism which was adapted to a backward society which had barely been exposed to the industrialism, the reformation, the intellectual awakening, and the general modernization of the West.

Communism has experienced, by virtue of a dia-
bolical combination of intrigue and military conquest,
a meteoric rise since World War II. At the Yalta Conference, in February, 1945, it was agreed that the
liberated peoples of East Europe would have restored
to them the sovereign rights of which they had been
deprived by the Nazis and would be free to form governments of their own choosing. One month later
Rumania, by the combined action of its internal Communist Party and Soviet troops, became the first of the
satellites. In September of that year, Bulgaria suffered
a like fate, in December, Albania. Hungary came next
in August of 1947, Czechoslovakia in May, 1948, and
Poland in January, 1949. By 1950, China had turned to
communism.

It is now obvious that Russia's expansionist ambitions
and communist China's lust for power have by no
means been satisfied. This is evidenced by Cuba and the
Congo, by Berlin and Viet Nam, and by many others.

The Characteristics of Communism

Materialism. Communism may be understood as a
political system with an economic base or as an economic system with a political body. It not only sub-
scribes to a thorough-going materialism; it is rooted and
grounded, conceived and gestated, born and lived out
in materialism.

The Marxist concept of the dialectic was adapted by
Karl Marx from the German philosopher Hegel. Hegel
reasoned that every force in life is in conflict with an
opposing force and that the resulting clash between
the two results in a combination of their original elements into a third new force. Marx believed that communism was the ultimate new force that would be in-

evitably created out of the conflict between labor and capital. His doctrine of economic determinism holds that the nature of society is determined by material forces and not by any supernatural force.

That Lenin learned this doctrine well is indicated by his often quoted statement, "There is nothing in the world except matter and its motion." For Communists there are but two competing systems, idealism and materialism. And materialism, they believe, is predestined to conquer!

Class hatred. The communist foe is characterized not only by materialism but also by a particularly virulent form of class hatred. He sees the clergy, the churches, the government, the courts, the whole legal system, and the various institutions of society all as parts of an elaborate system devised across the centuries by the ruling classes to exploit the laboring classes and to maintain power for themselves. He sees all human history as a series of social systems each of which has been based on a particular method whereby the capitalistic classes have exploited the laboring classes to maintain power for themselves. Marx declared in the *Communist Manifesto:* "Society is more and more splitting up into two great hostile camps, into two great classes directly facing each other: bourgeoisie and proletariat . . . .

"Let the ruling classes tremble at a Communistic revolution. The Proletarians have nothing to lose but their chains. They have a world to win.

"Working men of all countries unite!"

Truly a key feature of communism is its class consciousness, its class hatred (of the bourgeoisie), its class deification (of the proletariat), and its one great overriding goal of a "classless society." While Christian love is clearly one of the most significant ideas in Christianity, communism knows no such emotion. It knows hate. It hates capitalism and it hates capitalists. It hates freedom and it hates the United States. It hates Christianity and it hates Christians. One of communism's most glaring moral errors is its hatred.

Commitment to Revolution. Yet another characteristic of the communist foe is its commitment to revolution. The age in which Karl Marx was born and grew to maturity was one of the most radically revolutionary ages the world has ever known. When Karl Marx was a university student in his most impressionable years, Europe was boiling furiously with revolutionary plans, nihilistic schemes, anarchistic programs, and radical ideas of all kinds. The revolutionary notions which were common knowledge throughout Europe during the second decade of the nineteenth century became the special stock-in-trade of Karl Marx and the Marxists after him. In 1850 Marx hastily prepared an address to the Communist League in which he reminded his "brethren" that "their battle cry must be: THE PERMANENT REVOLUTION." Lenin's grasp of this concept of permanent revolution is evident. Said he in 1919: ". . . There are wars and wars. We condemned the Imperialist war, but we do not reject war in general. . . . Of course not. We are living not merely in a state, but in a system of states, and the existence of the Soviet Republic side by side with the Imperialist states for a long time is unthinkable. One or the other must triumph in the end. And before that end supervenes, a series of frightful collisions between the Soviet Republic and the bourgeois states will be inevitable." (Harry and Bonaro Overstreet, *What We Must Know About Communism,* p. 84.) Yet the Soviet rulers have recently staged a much-publicized return to Lenin who is represented as an exponent of peaceful co-existence! In spite of what some Communists now say, communism's commitment to permanent revolution must not be forgotten.

Ethics. As communism cannot be understood apart from its materialism, its class hatred, and its commitment to revolution, neither can it be understood adequately apart from its ethics.

Throughout his mature lifetime Karl Marx pursued his goal of the establishment of communism with an overwhelming Germanic single-mindedness. He flatly denied by example and by precept the existence of any ethical system or moral code that might in any way hinder or delay the communist take-over of the world. Lenin, consummate tactician of communism's moral zig-zag, summed up communist ethics when he declared, "We say that our morality is entirely subordinated to the interests of the class struggle." In communism the jesuitical doctrine that the end justifies the means has been developed into a science that makes the Roman Catholic Inquisition look like a little girl's tea party. All kinds of struggle, all means of promoting revolution, all violence, all compromise which could possibly work to communist advantage, and every type of conduct that will promote communism's cause are ethically acceptable to the communists.

The ethics to which communists give attention, the morality to which they subscribe, may exist; but the system is diametrically different from Christian ethics, from Christian morality.

Communism as a Religion. Another characteristic of communism is its strange appearance as a world religion. Communism does not recognize the existence of a supreme being. It does not believe our Bible. It denies the Christian claim that Jesus Christ is God's son. It has no place in its system for the church. It looks forward to no heaven and it fears no hell. Yet communism is itself a religion in the sense that it is *the* thing around which millions of communists orient all their endeavors. The communist regards communism as the ultimate good. He trusts it unconditionally for salvation from the evils of life. He finds in it meaning for his existence. In it he discovers the authority which, in some form, every man must have. The writings of Marx and Engels and Lenin constitute a body of sacred literature for communists. They have their own atheistic brand of predestination. Their worship is turned to the Party, to science, to education, and even to the body of Lenin. They have their saints whom they adore and their heretics they abhor. The coming to power of the proletariat, the working classes, is for them a sort of advent of a messiah. Personal property in communist thought is a kind of original sin. Their missionary enterprise is the carrying to all people of the "good news" of communism's release for the captives of capitalism.

The Rejection of the Worth of the Individual. Communism, moreover, has never had a place in its system for the Christian doctrine of the worth of the individual. Its thorough-going materialism has led it to reject this idea entirely. It is interested in classes but it is not concerned about persons. It professes to seek the good of society but it does not seek the good of individual members of society. It claims to want a free world but it has no place in its system for free men.

The Individual Christian and the Communist Challenge

The foe Christians face in communism is undoubtedly a fierce and formidable Philistine. When the individual

Christian comes to consider what he personally can do about communism, however, he is apt to feel frustrated if not completely helpless. What can the individual Christian do about communism if indeed he can do anything at all? He ought to take communism seriously for it is really far different from the political platform of nine-year-old Dale Smith, an English schoolboy who ran for a school office on the Communist Party ticket. His platform had three planks: (1) Give family income to children instead of parents. (2) Give free ice cream to all school children. (3) Hang all school teachers.

The Christian ought to think through the problems concerning communism. He ought to analyze its challenge. He ought to understand its appeals. He ought to comprehend its errors. He cannot afford to oppose it on the basis of blind prejudice. Christians must rather "by reason of use have their senses exercised to discern both good and evil" (Hebrews 5:14). He must examine communism's evil fruits and not be blinded by its empty talk. He must make a very special point of avoiding misinformation about communism. A thousand voices clamor to be heard on this subject today but many of them spout out tragic misinformation.

One thing is certain. The Christian must not succumb in impotent fear before the communist threat. Contrary to what the extremists are saying, every communist is not ten feet tall, every free man is not a dupe, and the Communist Party has no inexorable, inviolable, immutable timetable before which all mankind must tremble and fall by 1973. It is true that Khrushchev once said he would bury us, but it took him eight years to bury Stalin. Consider the magnitude of communism's problems: the massive ideological split between the USSR and China; the spectacle of Mao Tse-Tung's rebuking first Khrushchev and then Kosygin; the booming economic achievements of the Free World, the Common Market, the Berlin Wall; Russia's hasty retreat from direct military involvement in Cuba; the solidity of Latin America's opposition to communism in Cuba; the inability of communism to get a foothold in Africa; and the gradual reinstatement of capitalist methods throughout much of the communist world. Finally, to make matters worse, it is reported that a thief broke into the Kremlin and stole the results of next year's free elections. No, every communist is not ten feet tall, every free man is not a dupe, and the communists enjoy no divine ordination to rule the world. The Christian need not—must not—waste his energies in fear.

The most important single thing that an individual Christian can do is to take Christianity seriously. The best defense against communism is the good offense of a sound and vigorous faith in Jesus Christ. Such commitment to Christ is necessarily personal. It cannot be broad and general. Nor can it be a national thing. By the very nature of things, Christianity as such cannot war against communism as such. The struggle has national and international aspects, to be sure; but it is at the personal level where both Christianity and ultimately communism must be tested and proved.

A personal, genuine commitment to Christ inevitably has its larger social influence. If one takes Christ seriously it is impossible for him to condone injustice, defend prejudice, tolerate tyranny, or harbor hate. When Christ is the Lord of his life he lives under the divine imperative to let justice roll down as waters and righteousness as a mighty stream (Amos 5:24).

The individual Christian should be aware of the conditions which contribute to communism. A country is ripe for communism where ignorance goes unchecked by knowledge, where corruption is not overcome by honesty, where the poor are exploited by the rich, where the masses are oppressed by a privileged few, and where the church has rejected true Christianity as impractical, becoming a kept chaplain to the *status quo*.

It is not a sign of weakness but of strength to recognize that communism has some just criticism not only of capitalism but also of democracy and the churches. There is grave moral danger from materialism wherever it may rear its ugly head, from injustice however subtle may be its debilitating parasitism, and from the manipulation of people no matter how desirable the end result may appear to be.

The individual believer has an awesome responsibility and a tremendous opportunity to so live and work and act and witness as to cast an effective vote against both communism and the conditions which contribute to it. In the long run it is not going to be the most vocal anti-communist who contributes most to the defeat of this false religion. It is rather going to be the Christian who proves by his own deep commitment to Jesus Christ that Christianity is a way of life superior to communism's materialism. Such commitment carried by every Christian into every area and relationship of life is a sure cure for communism. There is no other cure.

The Christian can pray. He can pray for God to confound all the builders of modern towers of Babel. He can pray for God's intervention against every totalitarian regime. He can pray for the helpless millions who are caught in the currents of history and are being swept along without peace, without health, without food, and virtually without hope. And he can pray for those Christians who live under Communist regimes, remembering that throughout history Christians have never been dependent for the vitality of their religious experience on favorable political climates. As Daniel was faithful to God in Babylon, as Peter and John were loyal to Christ in spite of being forbidden by the magistrates to preach or teach at all in His name, and as Paul and Silas did not cease to bear their Christian witness even in jail at Philippi, so modern Christians behind iron and bamboo curtains can, against great odds, maintain their Christian faith. For them to do so, however, requires a great measure of God's grace and mercy. Let no Christian who is so fortunate as to live in freedom without any fear whatever of persecution from the state, sin against God by failing to pray for those unknown and uncounted modern heroes of the faith to whom has fallen in God's providence the infinitely more dangerous and difficult role of living for the Lord under communist regimes.

Communism offers no more serious challenge to individual Christians than the challenge to preach the gospel. To every Christian there is a way open for some effective proclamation of this gospel. If Christians will abandon the idea that they have Christ and let Christ have them, then we can find again our lost radiance. If we can recapture the spirit of New Testament Christianity, then the churches of today will develop a moral and spiritual thrust before which no false doctrine on earth can stand. Man's last best hope is not capitalism or democracy or the United States or the United Nations. Man's last best hope is Jesus Christ.

This communist foe faced by Christians is aggressive, informed, dedicated, and disciplined. Moreover it has been amazingly successful in a surprisingly brief time. The nature of communism is such that the believer's natural reaction to this godless materialism is one of horror and hatred. We may wish that by ignoring it, communism would go away and leave us alone. We may wish that by hating it, this evil specter would stop haunting our world. But horror and hatred and wishing are not enough.

The prophet Hosea declared, "My people are destroyed for lack of knowledge" (Hosea 4:6). The kind of knowledge which we are now trying to gain concerning communism is absolutely necessary if we are to oppose it successfully. The failure to discipline ourselves enough to gain this knowledge might well result in our destruction. "Woe to them that are at ease in Zion" (Amos 6:1) is an ancient warning with a particularly modern application. The communists may be expected to conquer those who do not have the knowledge and moral strength to withstand their false doctrine.

The ideological power of communism is awful; but the power of Christian truth is more awful still. Karl Marx and Lenin were remarkably able men whose genius for thought and organization are unquestioned; but Jesus Christ, God's only Son, is Lord forever. The Communist Party with some thirty-five million members throughout the world is a fierce and formidable foe; but the Christian church made up of the redeemed who know Jesus Christ as Lord has the word of the Savior Himself that the gates of hell shall not prevail against it. My concern is not that we are outnumbered; for communists do not outnumber Christians in the world today. My concern is that we shall one day stand before the Judgment seat of Christ and in shame be forced to confess to Him who has the print of nails in His hands that we were not outnumbered but outcommitted.

Let us determine to oppose communist falsehood with Christian truth; communist hate with Christian love; communist profession with Christian practice; communist revolution with Christian redemption; communist declarations with Christian demonstration; communist repression with Christian freedom; and communist dedication with Christian discipleship. Let us work tirelessly to translate the gospel into a language of word and deeds that all the world can understand. Let us outthink, outlive, outdo, and outdie the communists. Let us change the world!

As the conflict between communism and Christianity further unfolds, let us as Christians trust God supremely and fight the good fight. And in the raging conflict let us be careful to remember that "God hath not given us a spirit of fear; but of power, and of love, and of a sound mind" (2 Timothy 1:7) for this "battle is the Lord's" (1 Samuel 17:47).

CHAPTER 5

Christians and the Current Racial Crisis

For magnitude and complexity, no moral problem in this nation's history can hold a candle to the race problem. None seems likely to approach it in the near future. While the clouds of racial crisis at one level are receding, those at other levels are ominously advancing. Still other clouds churn and whirl and dip and soar with such dizzying diversity as to defy description.

The race issue is still the most divisive issue in American life. It is at once political, economic, social, cultural, moral, spiritual, and religious. Almost every aspect and phase of life in all these spheres has been somehow affected by the race problem. Any current consideration of Christianity and moral issues is compelled, therefore, to consider the race issue. This consideration of Christians and the current racial crisis is undertaken with the understanding that honesty requires it but that humility must permeate it. It would, indeed, be highly presumptuous to expect that more could be accomplished than the reflection of some random rays of light into what is a dismal, if not unfathomable, abyss.

Background Factors

A multitude of diverse factors have been at work for a long time in determining the present shape of the racial crisis. Some of the more important background matters must be considered prior to any attempt to understand the current situation, arrive at some kind of diagnosis, and consider the possibility of a cure.

The central fact in the history of the American Negro is slavery. Slavery is the basic and determinative factor in the great drama of Negro-white relationships in the United States. It was this malignant, evil thing that doomed the Negroes when they began to be brought to this country in chains from Africa as early as 1619, to a place of continuing discrimination and social inferiority even in a land that from its beginning made the bold profession that all men were born "free and equal." In their acceptance of human slavery, the founding fathers of both our political and religious institutions ate sour grapes. It is not surprising or unnatural that their children's teeth should still be set on edge.

Although there is a certain tendency for all people to grow away from their cultural roots and to drift from their historical moorings, that process of complete severance of practically all cultural and historical ties has been most remarkably complete in the lives of American Negroes.

Dr. Samuel Proctor, a distinguished American Negro churchman and educator, had an experience in Africa as an executive for the Peace Corps which forcefully illustrates this point. When he first arrived in Africa, he was frequently asked what African language he spoke. It was assumed that this English-speaking black man had maintained some dialect as his mother tongue. Gradually, however, he was able to communicate to

them the fact that there simply was no tribal or national affinity, no cultural connection, between a black
man who had been Americanized for some three hundred years and men of the same color in Africa. One
day he asked one of the domestic helpers where he got
his hair cut. "From a barber who comes around on a bicycle," was the reply. "How much do you pay for your
haircut?" asked Dr. Proctor. "Two shillings," said the
Nigerian. "Well, I pay four shillings downtown, and
I don't like the way they cut my hair. Will the man on
the bicycle cut my hair?" "Yes," came the reply, "He'll
cut your hair." "Will he cut my hair for two shillings?"
"No, master," said the African black man to the American black man, "He won't cut a white man's hair for
two shillings." The African correctly assessed the absolute break that had taken place in cultural continuity
so that he experienced no sense of anthropological unity
with this Negro American.

To end slavery and to settle rankling differences of
opinion which had been harbored for a hundred years
as to whether the states were sovereign or the nation
was, the war between the States was fought. This extremely bloody and deeply emotional conflict was finally resolved in favor of the forces against slavery and
for national sovereignty. The years of civil war were a
terrible drain on the resources of the entire nation but
especially on those of the South. Those depleted resources, which after one hundred years, have not yet
been replenished, have been a galling reminder of defeat to the vanquished. Because Negroes were the occasion of that War they have served in the intervening
years constantly to remind the South of defeat, suffering, cultural poverty, economic deprivation, the lost
cause of state sovereignty, and lost face. This war is in

some respects the truly central feature in the history of the nation. A multitude of uncounted songs and sayings and stories and jokes and folk ways have arisen which indicate the Negro is blamed for this tragic turn of events. After all he has been easier to see than abstract history. His houses have been easier to bomb than the White House. As one symbol of conquering authority, he could be rejected with impunity.

After the cessation of hostilities in the Civil War, the dominant whites assigned the Negro such a patently inferior status that his condition was little better than it had been before manumission. When conquering Yankee soldiers finished the work guaranteeing that the Emancipation Proclamation abolishing slavery was more than just a piece of paper, they left the South's cultural house empty and swept and garnished. So, the devil of racial segregation moved in quickly. While this devil was not worse than the first, he has proven himself the blood kinsman of slavery with many of the same bizarre, grotesquely sinful features. Moreover he has been an exceedingly hard occupant to evict from the premises. Segregation was essentially a caste system in which Negroes not only were tolerated but were found positively useful "in their place." This caste system carefully maintained the master-servant relationship with the Negro always in the servant role and the white always in the master role.

Segregation of Negroes was actually practiced, of course, prior to 1865. When slavery was abolished, however, the institution of segregation not only persisted but was greatly strengthened so that for all practical purposes it took the place of slavery. With the Supreme Court's Plessy vs. Ferguson ruling in 1896, the "separate but equal" doctrine of racial segregation received temporary legal shelter. Prior to 1900, Jim Crow laws requiring legal segregation were practically unknown. Within the next decade, however, such laws mushroomed throughout the South, reaching their ultimate absurdity in Atlanta where Jim Crow Bibles were provided for Negroes to swear on in court. This rapid social change was brought about by the same kind of white, establishment leaders who today caution temperance, patience, and deliberateness lest hasty obedience to the law upset their long traditions. Those traditions actually go back only about fifty years. Legal shelter for Jim Crow lasted, however, only a relatively short time.

The death blow was dealt to legal segregation on May 17, 1954, when the Court ruled that segregation in the public schools on the basis of race is unconstitutional. The 1954 ruling was by no means the radical innovation that some partisans have made it out to be. There were actually no less than 39 federal court decisions against segregation prior to the 1954 decision. The legal defense of racial segregation had been crumbling steadily for decades. The Court's unanimous decision in 1954 dealt it the legal stroke of death. Then the Civil Rights Act of Congress in 1964 put the legislative and executive branches of federal government as strongly against legal segregation as the federal judiciary. Without legal legs to stand on, the institution of racial segregation can not permanently endure.

The tragedy of racial segregation has been that it has sought solution of the race problem in the objective manipulation of Negroes rather than in subjective repentance, forgiveness, and restoration. The tragedy for white Christians is that multitudes of them still find themselves unable to face the moral evils of segregation and label it the sin that it is. Their failure to create a climate of Christian good will based on the weightier matters of justice, mercy, and love has left many Negroes convinced that the only avenue open to them for the redress of their legitimate grievances was a secular protest against the oppressive injustice of segregation.

Is there cause for encouragement in the fact that slavery gave way to segregation and that segregation is now giving way to prejudice? Perhaps so. We should not be unduly exalted, however, over progress from one anti-Christian posture to another anti-Christian posture. Behind all three of these—slavery, segregation, and prejudice—lurks the evil doctrine of racism. Racism has been defined as "the dogma that one ethnic group is condemned by nature to congenital inferiority and another group is destined to congenital superiority." [Ruth Benedict, *Race: Science and Politics* (New York: Viking Press, 1940), p. 153.] Racism maintains that the colored peoples are condemned by fate to hereditary inferiority, at best only imitative and inherently incapable of significant cultural achievement, and that the white race alone is destined to occupy the positions of leadership, creativity, and power in civilization.

The roots of this doctrine go back at least as far as the Crusades when white Europeans first came in touch with non-Christian people of color. The era of European colonization of the rest of the world following the Reformation and the Renaissance saw the great period of growth for the pernicious doctrine of racism. Without this racist doctrine of white supremacy whereby the white man philosophically, and profitably, assumed "the white man's burden" of exploiting, under the guise of civilizing, the colored peoples of the world, the program of European colonization could hardly have succeeded. While such books as Joseph Arthur Gobineau's

Essay on the Differences of Races which has been called the master textbook of racism, the writings of Nietzsche, and Hitler's *Mein Kampf* have helped to solidify the doctrine of racism, those volumes are not responsible for originating the doctrine. Neither can the blame be placed on the pitiful misinterpretation of the Scriptures which has claimed that "God, the original segregationist," put a curse on Ham, turned him black, and ordained that ever after his descendants should be "hewers of wood and drawers of water." The blame must lie somewhere between ancient man's original sin and modern man's love of money.

Still another background factor in the current racial crisis is the marked physical difference between Negroes and whites. While certain racial differences in noses, hair texture, cranial indexes, shin bones, and lip structures are observed by anthropologists, it is the skin color which more than any other physical characteristic sets the races apart. Black and white color considerations permeate the culture. White lies are permissible lies. Black sheep are bad sheep. White gowns symbolize purity. Black marks besmirch the record. Life wears white. Death wears black. White horses are for victory and plenty. Black horses are for defeat and famine. Thus black men subtly suffer in comparison with white men.

If the difference between black and white were not so pronounced as to be obvious to even the most casual observers, the race problem could hardly have survived, much less have grown to its present proportions. Color differences between whites and blacks are real today, but they are not as marked as they were when the Negro first arrived from Africa. Three hundred and fifty years of miscegenation with whites has appreciably lightened the skin coloring of most Negroes so that they are now, in fact, not black but brown Americans.

Perspectives on the Problem

Now that some of the background factors have been considered in an effort to understand the current racial crisis, it is in order to seek to gain some special perspectives regarding the problem. These perspectives will be sought by focusing on the white problem, the Negro problem, the political problem, and the church problem.

The white problem is brought into focus when it is observed that most whites simply do not look on Negroes as the same kind of human beings they themselves are. The Southern credo, "A Negro is a Negro and nothing more," is closely akin to the American dilemma in which lip-service is paid to the American ideal of equality and brotherhood while the ideal is largely ignored in daily affairs. The white problem has not been the original creation or the continuing monopoly of the rural South. The whites of the urban North have little cause for self-righteousness at the point of race. *Newsweek,* on October 21, 1963, carried the following report on the myths which whites still believe about Negroes:

> There is some point at which most white Americans draw the line at the prospect of closer association with Negroes. One conclusion that can be drawn from the patterns of prejudice is that the greater the suggestion of physical contact, the greater the white antipathy—and even revulsion. One reason seems to be that the image of the Negro in the white mind is a complex of unflattering stereotypes. Three out of four whites, for instance,

believe that Negroes, as a race, are less ambitious than whites; 71 per cent think they "smell different"; 69 per cent say that Negroes have looser morals; 49 per cent that they want to live on handouts; 44 per cent that they breed crime. One in three says Negroes are an inherently inferior race.

It is evident from this survey that most white people apparently still accept the utterly erroneous stereotype of the Negro as a humble, childlike, happy-go-lucky, indolent, carefree, unambitious, lazy, patient, sleepy, religious, Baptist-if-he-has-not-been-tampered-with being who would really much prefer not to have been prodded into the present revolution by outside agitators. There is little evidence that this stereotype is subscribed to only by white Southerners. Apparently it is far more commonly accepted throughout the land than was supposed prior to recent developments ranging from California housing to New York riots. The white problem has many facets, of course. These include such varied manifestations as the Ku Klux Klans, the White Citizens' Councils, restricted housing, job discrimination, social snobbishness, biased treatment of Negroes by white officers and courts of law, and white rejection of Negroes for membership on hospital staffs, in legal fraternities, and in professional organizations, journalism fraternities, and church membership. The white problem is indeed severe.

The Negro problem is likewise severe. Few whites understood, prior to the current crisis, the depth of seething resentment and smoldering hatred for "Whitey" which boiled behind the black man's smiling exterior. The deep store of impatience, alienation, anger, resentment, and hatred which have been building up in Negro Americans for centuries is expressed by James Baldwin in his book, *The Fire Next Time,* when he says, "To be a Negro in this country and to be relatively conscious is to be in a rage almost all the time."

In addition to the rage which often issues in hatred for whites, the Negro problem is compounded by the fact that Negroes in a predominantly white world often appear subconsciously to hate themselves. They hate the blackness which sets them apart from the majority, and the less sophisticated among them fight this high visibility with skin bleaches and hair straighteners. Although slavery has been gone a hundred years, the slave psychology lingers on, and Negroes hate the apathy and lethargy which help to constitute it. While a minority of Negro leaders seek to cultivate what they call their "Negritude," the majority are in too frequent touch with oppression to develop a very significant and respectable pride of race.

The Negro problem is also compounded by the fact that he feels, as James Baldwin has graphically put it, that nobody knows his name. He experiences no real identity. The Black Muslims dramatize this deficiency by adopting the letter X as a symbol of their lost names. This feeling of facelessness, of namelessness, of nobodyness is very near to the heart of the Negro problem. It is a major psychological problem which whites can help Negroes with but which in the last analysis will have to be confronted and conquered by Negroes who come to understand that in a democracy, and especially in the Church of Jesus Christ, everybody is somebody.

A perspective is also needed on the political problem in order to understand the current racial crisis. The

1954 ruling of the Supreme Court that segregation in the public schools on the basis of race is unconstitutional was followed by a ruling in 1955 that a "prompt and reasonable start toward full compliance" must be made "at the earliest practicable date," and "that the vitality of these constitutional principles cannot be allowed to yield simply because of disagreement with them." For ten years the federal courts have slowly but surely brought the force of the entire federal government behind these decisions so that more and more the message is getting through to rank and file citizens.

There was a strong feeling, particularly among members of the white, Southern establishment, that the Supreme Court had overstepped its bounds and that obedience to their interpretation of the Constitution was not mandatory. Congress had made no law, the reasoning went, and the Supreme Court had no right to make one. That line of reasoning was annihilated by the Civil Rights law of 1964. Congress, by an overwhelming vote, passed the most sweeping legislation in a hundred years to guarantee to Negroes their voting rights, access to public accommodations, use of public facilities, admittance to public schools, and employment opportunities.

A further perspective is gained by looking at the current racial crisis in the light of the church problem. The churches in general and the main-line denominations like the Baptists, Methodists, and Presbyterians in particular have been, and very largely still are, severely divided over the race issue.

If Southern Baptists, for instance, behave with marked tendencies toward neurosis whenever and wherever the issue of race relations arises, there is one hugely ample reason.

The Southern Baptist Convention was formed in 1845

by those who did not want to give up the evil institution of human slavery against which the moral sentiment of mankind was crystallizing. Dr. W. W. Barnes points out that the Alabama Baptist Convention meeting November 7-9, 1840, took cognizance of the growing abolitionist sentiment and appointed a committee of five who made the following recommendations: "(1) That abolitionism was unscriptural, was against the national constitution, was against the peace and prosperity of the churches, and dangerous to the permanency of the union; (2) that money should be withheld from the Board of Foreign Missions and from the American and Foreign Bible Society until Alabama Baptists were assured that these agencies had no connection with antislavery. The following resolution was adopted: 'Resolved, that if satisfactory information be not obtained upon this subject, we recommend the formation of a Southern Board, through which our funds may be directly transmitted.'" [W. W. Barnes, *The Southern Baptist Convention 1845-1953* (Nashville: Broadman Press, 1954), p. 23.] It is truly pathetic to see the same worn phrases and the same tired reasons being advanced by the same kind of prejudice one hundred years later.

Dr. Barnes further declares in his own words, "The formation of the Southern Baptist Convention grew out of the division in the Home Mission Society and in the General Convention (foreign missions) over the question of slavery." [*Ibid.* p. 12.] Negro slavery is not just a blot on the escutcheon of Southern Baptists. It is the Convention's original *raison d'etre*. This central fact in the history of the Southern Baptist Convention can, by God's grace, be overcome, for God's strength is ever made perfect in man's weakness (2 Corinthians 12:9) and God's treasures are ever received and carried in earthen vessels (2 Corinthians 4:7). The only hope for rising above this desperately serious handicap is to recognize it, repent of it, confess it, and begin to "bring forth fruits meet for repentance" regarding it.

Marks of the church's problem are further to be observed in the effect of racial prejudice on the evangelism and missions enterprises. Dr. C. E. Autrey, Director of the Division of Evangelism for the Home Mission Board of the Southern Baptist Convention, told Christian Life conferences at Glorieta and Ridgecrest in August of 1964: "I think the race issue and our attitude toward it is curbing evangelism as nothing else is. There are many contributing factors to the decline in baptisms in recent years, but I think the basic and major contributing factor is the race issue because I don't think you can love and hate with the same heart." [C. E. Autrey, "Evangelism, Missions, and Race," *Christianity and Race Relations* (Nashville: The Christian Life Commission, 1964), p. 7.]

In calling for an uncompromised Christian witness at the point of race relations, John and Virginia Mills, missionaries to Africa, said in an open letter, "We must remember that the vast majority of the world's peoples feel very strongly that racism is unfair and wrong. We know from personal experience after these sixteen years as missionaries in Africa that no religion which preaches or practices racism has any hope of success there. No amount of sacrificial giving or praying or sending of missionaries can compensate for failure at this point." ["An Open Letter to Texas Baptists," *The Baptist Standard* (July 24, 1963), p. 12.]

The Current Crisis

The revolt of the American Negro, beginning with the Montgomery bus boycott, has been something new under the American sun. Its most spectacular successes have been accomplished through nonviolent direct action. By this, it has sought to create such tension that the white majority who have consistently refused to negotiate with Negroes are forced to confront the issues of prejudice, discrimination, and racism. The movement's theme song is, "We Shall Overcome Someday." Its strongest leader, Dr. Martin Luther King, Jr., is a Baptist preacher, the son of a Baptist preacher, and the grandson of a Baptist preacher. Its forward strides in a few short years have been phenomenal when it is remembered that social change is nearly always measured in centuries, or at least in decades, and seldom in mere years. Its method is to break unjust laws openly and in a spirit of love with a *willingness to accept the penalty* so as to arouse the conscience of the oppressing community and effect the replacement of unjust laws. The movement is unquestionably related to the world-wide social crisis that has permeated every nook and cranny of the globe.

The current explosions have come as the irresistible force of rising Negro dissatisfaction with the caste system has met the immovable object of white majority satisfaction with the *status quo*. Whereas most whites have cautioned, "Wait," and some have cried, "Never," most Negroes have pressed for improved conditions, "Soon," and their leaders have cried, "Now." In opposition to those "moderate" whites who criticize nonviolent direct action as unwise and untimely, Martin Luther King, Jr., has poignantly stated the Negro's case:

I guess it is easy for those who have never felt the stinging darts of segregation to say wait. But when you have seen vicious mobs lynch your mothers and fathers at will and drown your sisters and brothers at whim; when you have seen hate-filled policemen curse, kick, brutalize, and even kill your black brothers and sisters with impunity; when you see the vast majority of your twenty million Negro brothers smothering in an air-tight cage of poverty in the midst of an affluent society; when you suddenly find your tongue twisted and your speech stammering as you seek to explain to your six-year-old daughter why she can't go to the public amusement park that has just been advertised on television, and see tears welling up in her little eyes when she is told that Funtown is closed to colored children, and see the depressing clouds of inferiority begin to form in her little mental sky, and see her begin to distort her little personality by unconsciously developing a bitterness toward white people; when you have to concoct an answer for a five-year-old son asking in agonizing pathos: "Daddy, why do white people treat colored people so mean?"; when you take a cross-country drive and find it necessary to sleep night after night in the uncomfortable corners of your automobile because no motel will accept you; when you are humiliated day in and day out by nagging signs reading "white" men and "colored"; when your first name becomes "nigger" and your middle name becomes "boy" (however old you are) and your last name becomes "John," and when your wife and mother are never given the respected title "Mrs."; when you are harried by day and haunted by night by the fact that you are a Negro, living constantly at tip-toe stance never quite knowing what to expect next, and plagued with inner fears and outer resentments; when you are forever fighting a degenerating sense of "nobodiness";—then you will understand why we find it difficult to wait. There comes a time when the cup of endurance runs over, and men are no longer willing to be plunged into an abyss of injustice where they experience the bleakness of corroding despair.

["Letter From Birmingham City Jail," p. 6, published by the American Friends Service Committee, Philadelphia, Pa., May, 1963, in pamphlet form.]

The concept of nonviolent direct action has now been seriously challenged by the more militant and socially irresponsible proponents of what has been called "black power." Feeding on Negro frustration, unemployment, poverty, and desperation, the newly emerging leaders of this philosophy pose a critically serious threat to improved race relations. Lacking positive Christian insights, they offer no realistic strategy for getting to the promised land. Their call to burn, destroy, and kill is an irresponsible call which challenges Christians to overcome it with Christian love and Christian justice.

Toward Redemptive Involvement for Christians

In Jean-Paul Sartre's "No Exit," three alienated people shut up together conclude that hell is other people. In the Christian community, however, all reconciled people gathered together in the family of the Father's divine intention understand that even heaven may be realized only in a web of relationships with other people. As there is a basic genealogical unity in humanity, so there is a peculiar spiritual unity in the church of Jesus Christ. White and Negro Christians are not shut up together by His harsh judgment. They are drawn together by His compassionate love.

To many careful observers, the current racial situation appears hopeless. They foresee alienation feeding on alienation, prejudice buttressed with prejudice, hatred fortified with hatred, and blood in the streets. The "gloom and doom" crowd sees, through essentially Marxian eyes, an impending racial Armageddon as races move menacingly toward one another past the point of no return. They envision only "a certain fearful looking for of judgment and fiery indignation" (Hebrews 10:27) as unrepentant sinners finally reap the horrible harvest of what they have sowed.

To those who are able to see the current racial situation through the eyes of Christian faith, however, there is hope. It is clear to these that the Christian ideal of brotherhood has not been obliterated by mankind's fuzzy vision of it or the church's inadequate, earthenvessel grasp of it. Christians strongly affirm that the sublime work of Christ in breaching the dividing wall of hostility between men has not been in vain. Responsible citizens continue to cherish the great political insights of this nation's founding fathers who dared to establish the republic on the proposition "that all men are created equal." Men of faith believe that all this is not an empty dream destined to fade away in the glaring, man-made, nuclear light of modern realities. It is rather, we verily believe, the essence of reality.

What can Christians do in this critically important area? Some specific suggestions are here in order. Learn the facts about race and racism. Study the nature of prejudice. Through the church, secure recommendations of a few good books on the subject and then buy those books and read them for the topic is far too important not to be informed about. Get acquainted with individuals of other races and classes, making a continuing effort as a Christian to understand each one as a person and to love each one individually as you do yourself. Avoid the paternalism which treats another as a thing and not really as an individual. In conversation shun those categorical stereotypes which subtly downgrade those of other races or nationalities. Follow the wise counsel of James to let your speech be without offense in conveying prejudice, fomenting strife, expressing hate, or encouraging hostility. Bear positive Christian witness concerning the worth of every man before God, remembering that the basic Bible truth concerning the worth of the individual will never be generally applied to the victim of prejudice unless the doctrine is spelled out in concrete and minute detail. Oppose those unprincipled and unscrupulous people in public life who seek to exploit the racial situation for their own political purposes. Support legislators who are faithful to Bible teachings and Christian insights concerning race relations. Encourage your church to preach and practice the truly reconciling gospel of Jesus Christ bearing in mind that there is no other ultimately satisfactory solution to the racial ills that beset mankind. Lend your influence, contribute your money, and give your time for the solution of specific racial problems that arise in the community. Recognize the deep economic and social roots from which racial problems grow and work somehow daily against the survival of those poisonous roots. Take the initiative against the race problem, not against people, remembering that the goal is not increased bitterness but expanding Christian brotherhood.

What can Christians do about race prejudice? Be the church and preach the gospel.

So we hear and begin to understand when God says to us, as He did to Cain, "Where is your brother?" So we hear and begin to understand when God asks us through Malachi, "Have we not all one father? hath not one God created us?" (Malachi 2:10). So we hear and begin to understand when Paul reminds us as he did the Ephesians that we who were all once far away from God are now brought near to one another and to Him through Christ who "is our peace, who hath made both one, and hath broken down the middle wall of partition between us" (Ephesians 2:13-14). So we hear and begin to understand the lesson God taught Peter so that he could say, "God hath shewed me that I should not call any man common or unclean" (Acts 10:28).

If God calls His people to a sacrifice of which they have not so much as dreamed in solving the racial problem, then let us bear the cross, if not gladly, then at least resolutely. The devil of racism will not be easily exorcised. Prayer and fasting, sacrifice and crossbearing, repentance and even the redemptive shedding of blood have been called for in the past. If the world stands, they will be called for again.

Let us determine that through legislation and through love, through work and through witness, through open doors and through open hearts, through repentance and through renewal, and through radical loyalty to the reconciling Christ and His reconciling Gospel, we will give ourselves to a redemptive witness in the realm of race. Who will deny that from the racial desert God can help His people to grow a garden? Who will argue that from the ashes of racial conflict God can help His people to bring forth beauty? Let Christians, therefore, face the current racial crisis with a sense of chastened optimism for this battle, too, is the Lord's (1 Samuel 17:47).

CHAPTER 6

The New Morality in Christian Perspective

On the windward side of Molokai I have squinted through a high-powered microscope to focus my eye in awe on the living organism that causes leprosy. Near the Sabine River bottoms of East Texas I have looked down in elemental terror at the crawling copperhead snake that has just plunged the deadly poison of its loathesome fangs into my veins. Over the jungles of Paraguay I have looked out of the airplane window in unspeakable dismay to see what happens when an engine swallows a piston. Under the beautiful bridges of Venice and on the high walls of Buenos Aires I have observed with fearful fascination communism's grim and sinister hammer and sickle, painted red garishly so that even those who speed may read. In Panama's primitive interior where the heat is stifling and the humidity overwhelmingly oppressive, I have winced at the sickening, sudden onslaught of a fearful food poisoning which has wracked my frame with rigors of unbelievably severe proportions. Across the face of the earth in my lifetime I have been an anguished witness, however, to something far more sinister than any of these things: the incredible proliferation of an all-pervading nerve gas of immorality. This immorality now increasingly threatens to engulf mankind.

The whole world is today morally adrift in a vast and formless sea of easy permissiveness. The ancient call of the libertine to "eat, drink, and be merry for tomorrow we may die" is echoed in Ernest Hemingway's popular code, "What is moral is what you feel good after, and what is immoral is what you feel bad after." The age-old notion that every man should be free to do that which is right in his own eyes is reflected by D. H. Lawrence, author of *Lady Chatterley's Lover*, who wrote: "My great religion is a belief in the blood, the flesh, as being wiser than the intellect. We can go wrong with our minds, but what our blood feels and believes and says is always true. . . . The real way of living is to answer one's wants." [Quoted by Arnold Lunn and Garth Lean, *The New Morality* (London: Blandford Press, 1964), p. 80.] This approach to morality could be lightly dismissed as too woefully irresponsible for attention if it were not so popularly accepted as to pose a real threat to great multitudes of human lives the world over.

Aldous Huxley has confessed, or at least has objectively explained, that many allegedly liberated people have rejected morality because they have viewed it as interfering with their freedom, thus actually denying that the world has any real meaning whatsoever. [Ibid. pp. 12-13.] Hugh Hefner, architect of a highly profitable empire which includes *Playboy* magazine and a chain of *Bunny* clubs, says, "I'm tremendously, completely fulfilled. I wouldn't trade places with any other human being alive now or in any past age." [Calvin Tomkins, "Mr. Playboy of the Western World," *The*

Saturday Evening Post (April 23, 1966), p. 98.] Seeing himself as a modern liberator, Hefner has championed a barnyard morality which is as essentially anti-sexual as it is utterly immoral.

In this hedonistic approach to morality, no moral imperative is recognized. No moral ideal is envisioned. No supreme good is accepted. There is no goal except to squeeze out of life the greatest possible amount of sensual pleasure. The theme song of the New York World's Fair becomes the theme song of life: "Walk away from every care. This is your fun time. You are entitled to it."

This sickness in society is not new. It is as old as mankind's primeval disobedience of God. It is reflected in Cain's murder of Abel, in Noah's drunkenness, in Moses' wrath, in David's adultery, and in Peter's lies. It is seen in the thought of Theodorus, a Fourth Century B. C., Cyrenaic philosopher who said that a wise man "may steal and commit adultery and sacrilege at proper seasons for none of these actions is disgraceful by nature if one can put out of sight the common opinion about them which owes its existence to the consent of fools." [Quoted by Jack W. MacGorman in "Playboy Philosophy Exposed," *The Baptist Program* (August, 1965), p. 17.] It is discovered throughout the pages of history in the senseless slaughter of the Crusades, the dreadful persecutions in the name of orthodox religion, the exploitation of the under-developed peoples of the world by European colonialists, the wretched institution of human slavery perpetrated primarily against Africans, the virtual extermination of the American Indians, the scandal and intrigue that from time to time have plagued most of the governments of the world, the burning of witches, the imprisonment of bread-winners unable to pay minor debts, the punishment by death of the poor who stole food for their hungry children, the exploitation of children during the early years of the industrial revolution, and a multitude of other such morally grotesque enterprises as have always beset this buzzing Babel.

Demonstrably, immorality is not new. There are indications, however, that it is manifesting itself in modern times on an unprecedented scale.

While it is bad enough for the world to be morally adrift, it is far worse for Christians to be blown about by every wind of moral doctrine. For, as Chaucer asked, "If gold rust, what shall iron do?" and as the Apostle Paul put it, "If the trumpet give an uncertain sound, who shall prepare himself to the battle?" (I Corinthians 14:8). Christians are deeply concerned that too often the church is characterized by moral conformity to the world instead of moral transformation in it. What can be done to enable the people of God to get their needed moral bearings, re-chart their moral course in line with God's will as revealed by Christ and as enlightened by the Holy Spirit, and to begin to steer not only the vessel of their own lives but also the ship of human affairs, in which they travel together with the rest of mankind, toward the distant, but not obliterated, shore of Christian morality?

A spate of articles, books, lectures, sermons, talks, and lessons have flooded the land in recent months about the need for a new morality geared to the needs of modern men. What is this so-called "new morality"? John A. T. Robinson, Anglican Bishop of Woolwich, is the chief popularizer of the term; but, as he points out, ". . . It is not my phrase at all, but the Pope's—or rather that of the Supreme Sacred Congregation of the

Holy Office. It had in origin nothing to do with sex, but with existentialist or 'situational' ethics. As I used it, [*In Honest to God,* Chapter VI.] it was certainly no invitation to license but a plea for the most searching demands of pure personal relationship as the basis of all moral judgments." [John A. T. Robinson, *Christian Morals Today* (Philadelphia: The Westminster Press, 1964), p. 8.]

It is a pointless and profitless exercise to make the name, "new morality," a target of indiscriminate abuse. How much better it is to give careful consideration to the issues at stake in the new morality debate, to "try the spirits whether they are of God" (I John 4:1).

The "new morality's" supporters insist that they are not denying the importance of morality but are simply approaching it from the standpoint of persons instead of principles. They observe that the old emphasis on principles, codes, systems, and commandments has been notorious in its failure to produce genuine morality. They are convinced that if morality is achieved it must be achieved as every person decides for himself what is right. They believe that their ideas of freedom and personal involvement in making decisions can result in a more responsible morality than can ever be achieved under the legalized propositions of the "old morality." They do not see themselves as making huge concessions to the spirit of the age but rather as representing a return to a proper understanding of the true meaning of morality for Christians. They observe that all moral systems have been inevitably amended by elaborate methods of exception and compromise so that the situation, not the standard, actually determines the moral actions. [For instance, most of the more vigorous opponents of "situation" ethics or the "new morality" would

insist that the Ten Commandments constitute an absolute standard for mankind. Yet when confronted with
the absolute of the sixth commandment, "Thou shalt not
kill" (Exodus 20:13), and the modern moral issue of
capital punishment, they are generally agreed that the
situation of murder or rape calls for an explanation of,
and a departure from, what the commandment actually
says. A casuistry is thus evolved which works not only
for Roman Catholics but also for Methodists and Baptists.] They view puritanical codes as a signally unsuc-
cessful effort to establish again the burdensome legalism
which God in his grace abolished in Christ.

Advocates of the "new morality" affirm that the work
of Christ was at the very point of "blotting out the
handwriting of ordinances that was against us, which
was contrary to us and took it out of the way, nailing
it to the cross" (Colossians 2:14). They refuse "to treat
the Sermon on the Mount as the new Law." [John A. T.
Robinson, *Honest To God* (Philadelphia, The Westminster Press, 1963), p. 110.] They are, at this point,
in complete agreement with the most conservative,
orthodox, and evangelical Christians. As one of their
chief spokesmen says, they "insist that situation ethics
is willing to make full and respectful use of principles,
to be treated as maxims but not as laws or precepts
. . . . Principles or maxims or general rules are *illumi-
nators*. But they are not *directors*. The classic rule of
moral theology has been to follow laws but to do it *as
much as possible* according to love and according to
reason . . . . Situation ethics, on the other hand, calls
upon us to keep law in a subservient place, so that
only love and reason really count when the chips are
down!" [Joseph Fletcher, *Situation Ethics:* The New
Morality (Philadelphia: The Westminster Press, 1966),

45115

p. 31.] They believe that statutory morality robs men of their freedom under God, making of them less than God intends free men to be. They feel that utter frustration will follow if the Bible is turned into a rules book.

In the words of Bishop Robinson, ". . . To the 'old morality' it *looks* as if the advocates of the 'new' are betraying the absolutes of right and wrong and selling out to relativism. What I would seek to urge is that they have equally vital concern for the element of the unconditional but are placing it elsewhere. Jesus's purpose was to call men to the Kingdom of God, to subject everything in their lives to the overriding, unconditional claim of God's utterly gracious yet utterly demanding rule of righteous love. And men could not acknowledge this claim without accepting the constraint of the same sacrificial, unself-regarding *agape* over all their relations with each other. It is this undeviating claim, this inescapable constraint, which provides the profoundly constant element in the distinctively Christian response in every age or clime. For it produces in Christians, however different or diversely placed, a direction, a cast, a style of life, which is recognizably and gloriously the same. Yet *what* precisely they must do to embody this claim will differ with every century, group and individual." [*Christian Morals Today*, op cit. pp. 11-13.]

To sum up, advocates of the "new morality" or of "situation" ethics affirm that the moral constancy which the human race needs is found in the constancy of the foundation of God's law, not in the permanence of the superstructure. [*Ibid.*, p. 18.] They understand that Christians are not in the world with changeless principles to *apply* to an alien process but that God in Christ is in history so that Christians live with His assurance "not of a fixity impervious to change, but of a faithful-ness promising purchase over it." [*Ibid.*, p. 19.] They declare that "this 'new morality' is, of course, none other than the old morality, just as the new commandment is the old, yet ever fresh, commandment of love." It is what St. Augustine dared to say with his *dilige et quod vis fac,* which as Fletcher rightly insists, should be trans-lated not 'love and do what you please', but 'love and *then* what you will, do." [John A. T. Robinson, *Honest To God,* op. cit., p. 119.]

If one reads Bishop Robinson, Joseph Fletcher, and certain other advocates of the "new morality" very care-fully he is likely to conclude that these men are trying to recapture a significant Christian insight about the nature of morality for Christians. They very properly seek to avoid a graceless legalism which denies that be-lievers are gloriously, but responsibly, set free in Jesus Christ. Yet they sometimes come perilously close, in their actual facing of moral decisions, to a formless, bridleless, characterless moral anarchy at the brink of which moral man always stands. It is an extremely sophisticated and highly spiritual individual, indeed, who never needs any outside help in determining the nature and demands of Christian love in the specific moral decisions of life. As the law, according to Paul's understanding, was a schoolmaster to bring men to Christ, so the Bible's limited formulation of moral prin-ciples must properly be understood as useful agents in leading men to know and do God's will in their lives. No convincing case has yet been made for parents not to teach their children the specific Ten Commandments as well as the general, everlasting truth that is behind them. No convincing case has yet been advanced to abolish the laws which men have developed in codified form as a minimal moral standard within which civilized people must operate. Man not only needs concrete advice on specific moral decisions; he must have concrete support for moral choices if he is to achieve true morality.

It is difficult to go far into an effort to understand the "new morality" without concluding that the proponents generally manifest a serious disregard for the tragic realities of human sin and the wretched depths of human degradation. In heaven their theory should work perfectly; but on earth it slips easily, if not inevitably, into a convenient anti-nomianism or an untenable moral nihilism. It is hard to escape the damaging conclusion that their followers, less theologically oriented than they, are much more likely to become immoral misfits than they are to find places of leadership as moral men in a moral society. Students are notably prone to draw the conclusions which their teachers are often willing to do no more than imply. These students of little faith or no faith at all, distant followers, misinterpreters, and perverters of the "new morality," holding to a playboy philosophy of morals, know nothing and care less about God's call to true Christian morality.

Soren Kierkegaard said, "Christianity begins with the doctrine of sin." It is also true that Christian morality must begin with the doctrine of sin. Where there is no sense of God's ideal for men, there can be no sense of missing that mark; and where there is no sense of missing His mark in life, there can be no sense of forgiveness, no knowledge of restoration, and no experience of renewal in Jesus Christ.

Is the old morality out of date? Are the Ten Commandments meant for the past and the Sermon on the Mount for the future, as some insist?

The answers to these questions are not difficult for Christians to find. God is good. He is upright. He is pure. He is honest. He is just. He is moral. Moreover, His call to sinful man is not an abstract call to a vague psychological, theoretical redemption of the shadowy substance men call the soul. His call is rather a specific, concrete call to the salvation of the total personality— body, mind, and soul. It is a call to goodness, to uprightness, to purity, to honesty, to integrity, to holiness, to wholeness, to righteousness, to morality. God makes it clear that His grace redeems man without man's *doing* anything. This explicitly does not mean, however, that man can do *anything* and still be a Christian.

Because God is deeply, creatively, and everlastingly concerned about morality, His people must maintain a creative interest in morality, being careful to separate the wheat from the chaff in the modern debates that are raging on every hand about the subject.

The word "morality" comes from the Latin *mores,* meaning manners, custom, tradition, habit. A related word, "ethics," is derived from the Greek *ethos,* meaning custom, habit, disposition. Neither word is found in the King James' translation of the Bible although *ethos* occurs rather frequently in the original texts. Yet, the Bible is the inspired record of a moral God dealing with morally responsible men.

Emil Brunner introduced his book, *The Divine Imperative,* which he called a "Protestant Ethic," with this declaration: "The question, 'What ought we to do?' the great question of humanity, is the entrance to the Christian Faith; none can evade it who wish to enter the sanctuary. But it is also the gate through which one passes out of the sanctuary again, back into life." [(Philadelphia: The Westminster Press, 1947), p. 9.]

Christians must begin to concern themselves far more seriously with this question, What ought we to do? and with the question, Is it right or is it wrong? Sophisticated modern man may wish to evade these questions; but, by virtue of his creation after the likeness of moral God, he simply cannot succeed in such evasion.

The Ten Commandments present an early formulation of God's requirements concerning morality in the lives of His people. The first table of the Law, relating man properly to God, constitutes the foundation upon which rests the second table, relating man properly to his fellowmen. Mankind has never outgrown, nor will mankind ever outgrow, these moral standards: "Honour thy father and thy mother. Thou shalt not kill. Thou shalt not commit adultery. Thou shalt not steal. Thou shalt not bear false witness. Thou shalt not covet" (Exodus 20:12-17). Modern man is in deep moral trouble today not because this moral code is irrelevant in the Twentieth Century. He is in grievous trouble because he has ignored God's great and changeless moral law. Thinking he could break this law with impunity, he has instead broken himself upon it.

The New Testament provides a more fully developed call to morality for God's people than is found in the record of His dealing with the ancient Jews. Although it is not essentially different from that of the Old Testament, it is actually more rigorous, more demanding, more thorough. Christ's coming did not destroy or nullify God's moral law. Rather, it fulfilled it. The New Testament does not present a glowing and imaginative description of morality. It rather presents a living ideal in the presence and person of Jesus Christ.

Boris Pasternak speaks movingly to this point in *Doctor Zhivago* when he has Nikolai Nikolaievich to write in his diary: "Rome was a flea market of borrowed gods and conquered peoples, a bargain basement on two floors, earth and heaven, a mass of filth convoluted in a triple knot as in an intestinal obstruction. Davians, Herulians, Scythians, Sarmatians, Hyperboreans, heavy wheels without spokes, eyes sunk in fat, sodomy, double chins, illiterate emperors, fish fed on the flesh of learned slaves. There were more people in the world then than there have ever been since, all crammed into the passages of the Coliseum, and all wretched.

"And then, into this tasteless heap of gold and marble, He came, light and clothed in an aura, emphatically human, deliberately provincial, Galilean, and at that moment gods and nations ceased to be and man came into being—man the carpenter, man the plowman, man the shepherd with his flock of sheep at sunset, man who does not sound in the least proud, man thankfully celebrated in all the cradle songs of mothers and in all the picture galleries the world over." [Boris Pasternak, *Doctor Zhivago* (New York: Signet Books, 1957), p. 40.]

God has, indeed, manifested in Jesus Christ the moral perfection toward which mankind ought to be constantly striving. His perfect moral life, moreover, is an encouragement and an ideal to those who have heard His call to follow Him. His exemplary moral life is not so far removed from the human situation as to cause mere men to despair. Christ's stringent, demanding "Be ye perfect" (Matthew 5:48) is not a command to achieve an obviously impossible sinless perfection. It is rather a powerful reminder for Christians of every age to keep on striving toward moral wholeness, toward practical righteousness, toward the good life.

No clearer, more precise summary or distillation of

the essence of Christian morality is to be found than that presented in the dramatic dialogue between Jesus and the lawyer. The lawyer asked, "Master, which is the great commandment in the law?" Jesus answered, "Thou shalt love the Lord thy God with all thy heart, and with all thy soul, and with all thy mind. This is the first and great commandment. And the second is like unto it, Thou shalt love thy neighbour as thyself. On these two commandments hang all the law and the prophets" (Matthew 22:36-40). Paul's understanding of this same insight led him to write, "For all the law is fulfilled in one word, even in this; Thou shalt love thy neighbor as thyself" (Galatians 5:14). Thus, the basis of Christian morality is seen to be unqualified love for God, and the manifestation of Christian morality is seen to be a love for others that is as deep and wide as the love of life itself.

This love for God and for mankind is not primarily an emotion or a fond affection. It is rather basically a volitional commitment, a positive determination of the will, to seek the good of others. The opposite of Christian love is not hate but indifference. Christian morality does not require us to feel a warm affection for everybody. It simply requires us to deal lovingly with all with whom we have any dealings at all. Moral actions are not performed in obedience to outward laws but in obedience to the demands of the indwelling Christ.

Without such love there simply can be no Christian morality no matter whether rules are slavishly followed or sophomorishly thrown overboard. As Paul Tillich put it, ". . . Without the imminence of the moral imperative, both culture and religion disintegrate because of lack of ultimate seriousness." [*Morality and Beyond* (New York: Harper and Row, 1963), p. 19.] While

Christ Jesus gives ultimate seriousness to this issue of morality, he does so with great grace and the assurance that in the realm of morals his yoke is easy and his burden is light (Matthew 11:29-30).

Many admirably moral people make no profession of religion in general or of Christianity in particular. They make a sincere and often successful effort to do unto others as they want others to do unto them. Not all moral men are Christians, but all Christians are moral men. While Christians have no monopoly on morality, Christian morality has significant distinctives.

Christian morality finds its origins in the encounter between God and man whereby God's grace and man's faith come together in such a way as absolutely to transform human life and subsequent human relationships. The Christian's love for others, the essence of Christian morality, is no mere psychological stance. It is rather a warmly compassionate, sacrificial good will expressing itself redemptively in the Christian's everyday life.

Christian morality is both personal and social. It is first personal in the sense that the Christian accepts the Lordship of Christ in every area and relationship of his personal life. It is then social in the sense that the Christian understands his responsibility to be his brother's keeper as he walks daily in the moral light of God in Christ. Christian morality is an inward reality which inevitably seeks and invariably finds meaningful outward, social expression.

Morality never saved anyone, but anyone who is saved by God's grace through repentance and personal faith in Jesus Christ seeks throughout the pilgrimage of his Christian life to achieve and manifest that true Christian morality which is the fruit of the Spirit.

God gives many good gifts to His people, but none is more significant than the gift of the indwelling Spirit, who makes Christians like Christ in character. So, "Let us be Christ's man from head to foot, and give no chances to the flesh to have its fling" (Romans 13:14, Phillips).

CHAPTER 7

You Can't Go Home Again

In one of the most poignantly insightful titles in American literature, Thomas Wolfe makes the point that you can't go home again. The point is at once practical and profound, mundane and philosophical, somber and joyous, bitter and sweet, devastating and exhilirating. Most of us have tried it a thousand ways and know with Thomas Wolfe's George Webber, ". . . that you can't go home again."

". . . You can't go back home to your family, back home to your childhood, back home to romantic love, back home to a young man's dreams of glory and of fame, back home to exile . . . back home to lyricism . . . back home to aestheticism . . . back home to the ivory tower, back home to places in the country . . . back home to the father you have lost and have been looking for, back home to someone who can help you, save you, ease the burden for you, back home to the old forms and systems of things which once seemed everlasting but which are changing all the time—back home to the escapes of Time and Memory." [Thomas Wolfe, *You Can't Go Home Again* (New York: Harper and Brothers, 1941), p. 706.]

The Hebrew children spent forty fruitless and futile years trying to go home again, to what was in reality an alien land. Their experience is recorded with brilliant clarity in Numbers:

> "And all the congregation lifted up their voice, and cried; and the people wept that night. And all the children of Israel murmured against Moses and against Aaron: and the whole congregation said unto them, Would God that we had died in the land of Egypt! or would God we had died in the wilderness! And wherefore hath the Lord brought us into this land, to fall by the sword, that our wives and our children should be a prey? were it not better for us to return unto Egypt? And they said one to another, Let us make a captain, and let us return into Egypt" (Numbers 14:1-4).

For trying in her own faithless, circumscribed, feminine, human way to go home again, Lot's wife turned into a pillar of salt.

The wise man in Ecclesiastes was saying that you can't go home again when he said, "Say not thou, What is the cause that the former days were better than these? for thou dost not inquire wisely concerning this" (Ecclesiastes 7:10).

T. S. Eliot spoke with poetic precision when he had J. Alfred Prufrock to say, "I have seen the moment of my greatness flicker, and I have seen the eternal Footman hold my coat, and snicker, and in short, I was

afraid." There are signs that we, like Prufock, have
seen the moment of our greatness flicker, we have seen
the eternal Footman hold our coat and snicker, and in
short, we are afraid. This is a critical time for Christians
generally. We will forfeit the future if we continually
bathe ourselves in nostalgia and expend our energies in
vainly trying to go home again.

It is in order for us to focus briefly on the home from
which many of today's churches in the United States
have come.

We were a country people, but, like the rest of
America, we have moved to town.

We were an uneducated, even ignorant, people, but
we are now learning a few things.

We were a provincial people in confident control of
our province, but to our anguish and dismay our cogs no
longer seem to engage the gears of any real power in
our culture. We find ourselves an isolated and waning
force in the court house, the state house, the White
House, and the Glass House on the East River.

We were racially, historically, economically, politi-
cally, and culturally homogeneous, but we are fast
becoming irreversibly heterogeneous.

We were revival-oriented, but revivalism as known
and practiced when I was a boy is dead. It is dead in
spite of our frantic mouth-to-mouth breathing over it
and even though we still respectfully hold one-week
and even two-week memorial services in loving tribute
to its memory.

We were poor, but now, by any reasonable standard
on earth, we are rich.

We were ill-housed in our one-room, crowded, frame
meeting houses, but now we meet in splendid, un-
crowded sanctuaries for which we are gloriously in debt.

We were fervently convinced of the rightness of our cause, but now we harbor all the questions and doubts that normally accompany a measure of sophistication.

We were stoutly and vociferously opposed to the institutionalism of the old-line churches, but in only a hundred years we have established institutionalism of every shape, form, and fashion; and all the web is not yet woven.

We were rooted in the soil, but now from the cradle to the grave we roll around on the pavement.

We were a brash and lusty adolescent people bulging with unguided muscles, but the aging process has worked its unwelcome work on us and we are now politic, cautious, meticulous, respectable, proper, aging.

We lived in a settled, unchanging world where we knew even as we also were known, but now we live in a world where the winds of change blow with devastating fury across the face of all the earth.

We lived in an isolated, marvelously moated land where men never dreamed of mastering the black arts of nuclear war, but the time has come when men in a fantastically shrunken world have both dreamed that dreadful dream and actualized it.

This has been home. For us to go home again would be to go back to the country, back to ignorance, back to provincialism, back to radical sectarianism, back to homogeneity, back to revivalism, back to poverty, back to isolationism, back to our cabins in the clearings, back to the frontier, back to all this and much, much more.

Why are we trying to go home again? Because it is the natural thing to do. Because it is inevitable when growth has come. Because we can not help it when we have aged a bit. Because we are caught in a world in travail and we are badly disoriented. Because we have not yet found ways of adjusting to industrialism, unionism, urbanism, statism, socialism, or for the most part even capitalism. Because we have discovered that our old formulae for success are no longer producing results and we are in shock about it. Because we have not learned to speak today's tongue. Because we are really not at home in this brave, new world.

How are we trying to go home again? By reproducing country churches in the city suburbs. By resorting to the use of artificial stimuli to produce results like we used to have. By hiding the fact that while we are fierce of visage we are actually faint of heart. By maintaining the pretense that we are as brave as bulls when we have actually become as timid as mice. By cultivating a mood that says, "Hang the facts. Give me a cliché." By our compulsive activism.

What is going to come of the effort to go home again? The effort will win some battles but it will lose the war. It is not a mean and ignoble thing to try to go home again. In fact, it has certain truly sublime elements. It is simply not starred to succeed. We cannot turn back the clock or even stop it no matter how dramatic our histrionics. We cannot re-capture our past. We cannot recall yesterday. We can't go home again.

If we can't go home again, then where can we go?

Like Abraham, we must seek that city whose builder and maker is God. While the City is in eternity, the seeking must be done in time. Christ was teaching us something very near to the heart of His gospel, not just a bit of pretty ritual, when He taught us to pray. "Thy kingdom come. Thy will be done in earth, as it is in heaven" (Matthew 6:10). Believers are not free to flag or fail until "the kingdoms of this world are become the kingdoms of our Lord, and of his Christ" (Revelation 11:15).

While we can't go home again, we can move meas-
urably toward that true home which God is pre-
paring for them that love Him. Here and now, with
God's help and by His grace, we are to be moving con-
sciously, conscientiously, and consistently toward this
ideal home. Its final consummation we necessarily
await, but its distinct outlines and chief characteristics
we need already to be getting familiar with.

In order that we may neither waste precious time
in looking back at the home whence we have come or
in looking bewilderedly for the wrong city, let us give
attention to some of the distinctive features of our true
home, the City of God. Any home which is satisfying
and adequate for God's people here must approximate
in outline and foreshadow in form the qualities of the
home hereafter.

How can the eternal home be identified? What is
heaven like? Unto what shall the City of God be liken-
ed? It is a family. It is a brotherhood. It is a moral
fortress. It is a workshop. It is a kingdom. Let us
consider these characteristics.

The ultimate home which Christians seek is a family.
In it God is Father, Jesus Christ is elder Brother, and
the Holy Spirit is eternal Comforter. In it, the family
of God's redeemed children shall ever dwell together
in unity. The home we seek is characterized by love,
joy, peace, patience, kindness, goodness, faithfulness,
gentleness, self-control.

In view of that home which is our ultimate destination, let us, as an earnest of our intent, begin here and
now to make of our human homes little colonies of
heaven where we dwell together in Christian love,
Christian joy, Christian peace, Christian patience,
Christian kindness, Christian goodness, Christian faith-

fulness, Christian gentleness, and Christian self-control. If my profession of interest in the home to come is genuine, then there must be a reflection of that interest in my home housed on Torrington Road in Nashville.

The concept of family in our Christian faith eschews too-early dating, immature marriages, feminine fathers, masculine mothers, undisciplined children, absentee parents, juvenile delinquency, promiscuity, divorce, materialism, and all the other forces that fragment today's families. It is a concept that embraces careful preparation for marriage, spiritually solid foundations for marriage, and marriage that is both initiated and lived out "in the Lord," where believers are not yoked unequally together with unbelievers and where husband and wife and parents and children are so caught up in a dream bigger than themselves that they strive through the years to make the dream of a truly Christian home come true.

Christians seek a home characterized by brotherhood. It is a city without walls. Outside walls are not necessary in the home where we are headed because there are no enemies there. And inner walls are not required because the redeemed who dwell together in brotherly love have no selfish interests to protect, no evil to hide, no exclusiveness to relish, no psychological complexes to nurture by shutting out somebody else.

In view of the city without walls sought by the saved, it behooves us to begin here and now to build such cities of brotherhood. The middle wall of partition which still divides believers is a wall Jesus Christ died to tear down. To the extent that we worship that divisive wall, we re-crucify Christ. To the extent that we tolerate it, we deny Him who came to break it down. To the extent that we cherish it, we dishonor Him who hated it and who hates the pride and prejudice it still stands for.

To pretend that our prejudice in maintaining the walls of racial segregation, class consciousness, economic exclusiveness, and social snobbery does no violence to the gospel of Jesus Christ our Lord and the altar of God, our Savior, is to close our eyes to the real purpose of the life and death of Christ.

We need to abolish racial discrimination in our country and in our churches, not because of a clause in the Constitution, nor because of the communist challenge, nor yet because we need the votes of the watching world. We need to conquer race prejudice because it is a sin against almighty God and a rejection of the precious blood of Jesus Christ, His only begotten Son.

Let us then cease shouting at each other across Kipling's "seas of misunderstanding." Let us rather undertake to learn, in preparation for the brotherhood beyond, to call God, "Father," and all His people "Brother," so that God's city without walls begins to look attractive to us here and now.

Christians seek a home which is a moral fortress. It is that bastion of ultimate integrity, that impregnable mother lode of rectitude, that veritable quintessence of righteousness which John the Revelator described as the city where "there shall in no wise enter . . . anything that defileth, neither whatsoever worketh abomination, or maketh a lie" (Revelation 21:27).

As we seek the city "wherein dwelleth righteousness" let us "follow righteousness" on our way there. As we seek the city where no immorality in any form shall ever be, let us make our profession of religion a morally relevant and ethically meaningful thing here and now. Christian morality demonstrates its genuineness only when it authenticates itself outside the church house in the rough-and-tumble world in which we daily live.

In this world's moral gloom let us not idly tolerate the erosion of all moral standards until our churches become like Robinson Crusoe's goat pasture, so that the goats inside are as wild as the goats outside. Let us rather in the moral realm become "Christ's men from head to foot and give no chances to the flesh to have its fling" (Romans 13:14, Phillips).

Christians seek a home which is a workshop. The old rocking chair won't get us there. The notion that in heaven we will be stretched out on flowery beds of ease to do nothing forever has an unquestioned appeal when we are tired, but the fact is that the notion is extra-Biblical and grossly inaccurate. Our true home will be a place of creative and satisfying work for God where "his servants shall serve him" (Revelation 22:3).

As we seek the home which is the Christian's ultimate workshop, let us perform our daily work, here and now, "As unto the Lord." In the beginning God assigned Adam the work of tilling and keeping the Garden of Eden. In the decalogue He commanded His people, "Six days shalt thou labor." Even so He wills for us to work. Paul proclaimed this principle when he admonished, "If any one will not work, let him not eat" (2 Thessalonians 3:10, RSV). The Christian's approach to work involves seeking to find God's will concerning what work to do; experiencing something in the work itself which is significant before God and meaningful to man; cultivating a spirit of responsibility which takes honest pride in the work done; and in finding through daily work the highest self-development of which we are capable. Daily work, rightly understood, is no onerous chore but a holy task.

Christians seek as their permanent home the City of the Great King where our final citizenship is.

As we await the final papers for our future citizenship, let us honor that future with a significant Christian citizenship where we now live.

In the 1960 presidential election when interest in citizenship reached a new high, only 64.3% of the qualified voters in the United States bothered to go to polls. If we find corruption in government, we cannot honestly put all the blame on the so-called professional politicians. The blame must be shared by those who refuse to work in the normal processes of citizenship. In recent years many a good man has sought elective office only to be defeated by the apathy and inertia of his friends—equally good men who did not bother to get involved. Plato rightly said that the punishment suffered by the wise who refuse to take part in the government is to live under the government of bad men.

The Christian citizen recognizes that civil government is of divine appointment. He prays for those in positions of authority. He pays his taxes. He obeys the laws. He conscientiously casts his ballot. When the situation requires it, he presents himself as a candidate for public office. He remembers to use moral discernment in his support of governmental programs, bearing in mind that his ultimate loyalty is to the King of kings. The responsible Christian citizen will not even try to wash his hands of politics. He will rather try to get redemptively involved in the whole realm of citizenship.

If Christians bear clearly enough in mind the open portals of the eternal Home and hold well enough in focus the beckoning arms of the heavenly Father, then we will avoid both crippling commitments to the home of yesterday and debilitating compromises with the home of today. We must ride light in the saddle if we are to avoid injury when the horse stumbles. We must, if we are to manifest spiritual vigor and moral thrust, maintain a structured tentativeness with regard to this present age. Indeed, "It is people for whom the navel cord of this world has been cut who can give themselves most joyously to its redemption." [Karl A. Olsson, *Passion* (New York: Harper and Row, 1963), p. 91.]

This does not mean, however, that we are to retreat into stained glass sanctuaries, cutting off all concern for and commerce with the world. Quite the contrary. If we fail to leaven the lump, we fail Christ.

This emphasis on the Christian's responsibility in this world is based on the understanding that God Himself cares about what happens on this earth. Jehovah God was portrayed by the prophets as being concerned about such things as military alliances, the selling of debtors into slavery, the plundering of the poor by the rich, the cheating of the buyer by the seller, and the oppression of the weak by the strong. The God of the Bible, the God Christians know through personal faith in Jesus Christ, is no abstract First Cause or Prime Mover or Great Unknown out in the Great Somewhere who can be placated by a bit of discreet crying in the chapel. He is a personal God who is very deeply and very definitely concerned about military alliances, racial segregation, the unconscionable profits of the drug industry, the indefensible price fixing that honeycombs big business, and the criminal corruption that persists in organized labor. He is concerned about tax evasion, padded expense accounts, the exploitation of violence as entertainment, the toleration of senseless killings in the boxing ring, family fragmentation, and the unsolved problems of the aging. He is concerned about the unemployment which has been almost six per cent of our labor force in recent years, (the U. S. lost more time in one recent year from unemployment than we lost in the past thirty-five years from strikes) and the one hundred billion dollars a year (or about eight per cent of its gross annual product) which the world now spends on weapons. He is concerned about the hideous inanities preached as a sorry substitute for the Christian gospel, the infuriatingly bland and crashingly dull church programs calculated to produce an attitude of profane indifference, the immensely absurd spectacle of loving the souls of Negroes in Africa and hating their guts in America, and all the other moral flotsam and spiritual jetsam that could be orchestrated into this melancholy tune.

God cares, God is concerned. And since God is concerned, His people have an obligation to be concerned, too.

The demand of Christ our Lord is not that we should take a sentimental journey back home. It is rather a demand for us to take a bold and visionary giant step toward our Christian destination. What God wants of us today is not an eviscerated, all-things-to-all-men, formal confession of creedal correctness. What He wants is a quality of life that demonstrates to this world and to the great cloud of witnesses above that we have been with Jesus.